A Manual of English for the Overseas Doctor

Joy Parkinson BA
Former Head of Department of English,
Southwark College, London

FOURTH EDITION

CHURCHILL
LIVINGSTONE

EDINBURGH LONDON MELBOURNE NEW YORK AND TOKYO 1991

CHURCHILL LIVINGSTONE
Medical Division of Pearson Professional Ltd

Distributed in the United States of America by Churchill Livingstone Inc.,
650 Avenue of the Americas, New York, N. Y. 10011, and by associated
companies, branches and representatives throughout the world.

First Edition 1969
Second Edition 1976
Third Edition 1985
Fourth Edition 1991
    Reprinted 1992
    Reprinted 1993
    Reprinted 1994
    Reprinted 1996

ISBN 0-443-04188-1

British Library Cataloguing in Publication Data
A catalogue record for this book is available from the British Library

Library of Congress Cataloging in Publication Data
Parkinson, Joy.
    A manual of English for the overseas doctor/Joy Parkinson. – 4th ed.
        p. cm.
    Includes index.
    ISBN 0-443-04188-1
    1. Medicine-Language.   2. English language – Textbooks for foreign
speakers.   3. English language-Conversation and phrase books (for
medical personnel)   4. Medicine-Great Britain.   I. Title.
    [DNLM: 1. Medicine – phrases.   W 15 P247m]
    R123.P37   1991
    610'.14–dc20
    DNLM/DLC
    for Library of Congress

Produced by Longman Singapore Publishers (Pte) Ltd
Printed in Singapore

Contents

Preface to the fourth edition   vii
Acknowledgements to the fourth edition   ix
Preface to the third edition   xi
Preface to the first edition   xiii
Special note on weights and measures   xv

1 The structure of the National Health Service   1
2 The organisation of a hospital   7
3 Postgraduate medical training and registration   15
4 Letter writing   27
5 Case histories   51
6 Medical abbreviations   157
7 Descriptive language of systems review   171
8 Colloquial English: 189
   Parts of the body   189
   Bodily functions   192
   Mental and physical states   195
   Diseases and other conditions   197
   Reproductive organs and sexual problems   201
9 Phrasal verbs   207
10 Idioms   241
11 Language of dentistry   265
12 Language of drug addiction   271

Preface to the fourth edition

By no means all authors have the opportunity of discussing their books with their readers. Since the third edition of the Manual was published in 1985 I have had the opportunity of meeting many doctors from different parts of the world. They were able to indicate the changes they thought would be helpful in the fourth edition. Unfortunately, not all of them have been incorporated into this book otherwise it would have been twice the size.

Phrasal verbs are a perennial problem and this chapter has been completely rewritten with new examples, many of them from authentic case histories. Tests follow each phrasal verb.

Language is a living thing; it grows with new developments, increases as knowledge expands; it changes to reflect attitudes in society. One of the striking changes in the English language in recent years is that there is a strong tendency to use informal and colloquial language much more. Topics and words to describe them, once considered offensive, are now used widely by educated people. This means that overseas doctors must widen their knowledge of colloquial language in order to understand their patients. Chapters dealing with colloquial language, idioms and medical abbreviations have all been updated. The examples of language used in systems review have been expanded.

In the medical sphere, the profession has recognised AIDS as a pandemic. This being so, a detailed case history of an AIDS patient has been added. The decision to retain the case histories of earlier editions has been made for two reasons. Most doctors consider the detailed interviews of doctors and patients as one of the most helpful chapters of the book. A cassette recording of these case histories can be obtained from Tutor Tape. This enables doctors to practise listening comprehension with varieties of spoken English while in their own countries. This chapter is invaluable material for preparing for the 'listening in context' part of the PLAB test.

Finally, drastic changes in the NHS necessitated modifications and new material.

It is hoped that all these amendments and additions will make an even more informative book for you all.

London, 1991   Joy Parkinson

Acknowledgements to the fourth edition

As with the three previous editions of the Manual, I have had to turn to many people for the necessary specialist help.

I was advised on the language of drug addiction by Dr H Swadi of the Department for Child and Family Consultation, Medway Health Authority. Doug Young of the English Department, Southwark College, gave helpful advice on special vocabulary. Dr J Wood, Director of the Medical Department of the British Council, kindly assisted with the revision of the material on postgraduate medical training.

Most of the help, however, came from countless people at the Whittington Hospital; secretaries, librarians, doctors, all busy people, but appreciating the fact that overseas doctors coming to the UK for further training and experience do need help.

I should like to thank the following, therefore, for advice, encouragement and permission to publish information and case histories: Dr F Godlee of the Rheumatology Department, Dr D Grant of the Department of Imaging, Dr C Katona of the Department of Psychiatry and UCMSM, Mr I G Kidson, Unit General Manager, Dr D H L Patterson of the Cardiac Department and Dr L Raistrick of the Dermatology Department. Thanks are also due to Miss Sonia Hyde, Director of Nursing Services, for help with revision of the information on nursing staff. My special gratitude must, however, go to Dr Eric Beck, Consultant Physician at the Whittington Hospital.

He not only gave up time to answer my many queries but also put me in touch with all the other doctors without whom this new edition could not have appeared.

My thanks to Miss Zena Austin for so patiently typing the new material.

Preface to the third edition

Nothing remains the same for long. Structures of society and institutions change and these changes are reflected in language. So there is a real need for a new edition of the Manual. Every chapter of the book has been revised and updated; some parts have been pruned, others have grown.

The most significant event for many overseas doctors since the publication of the second edition was the introduction of the PLAB test (Professional and Linguistic Assessments Board). The aim of the test is to ensure that the overseas doctor has an adequate knowledge of medicine and English before being employed in the medical field in the United Kingdom. One of the most serious language problems is that patients do not speak the English of medical text books. Nor should doctors communicate to their patients in that technical language. So a real effort has to be made to learn some colloquial language. The case histories in Chapter 5 are an invaluable aid to the overseas doctor. New ones have been added. (A cassette of the case histories is available from Tutor Tape Company, London House, 68 Upper Richmond Road, London, SW15 2RP.) The chapter dealing with descriptive language is also vital for good doctor communication. Phrasal verbs and idiomatic English are difficult but necessary for a mastery of English.

We continue to prepare doctors for the PLAB test at courses at Southwark College in London. The more one teaches, the more one learns. In particular, one realises more and more how difficult it is for a doctor from overseas to communicate in English with a patient from a totally different cultural background. So in this new edition an attempt has been made to be more explicit, to give better, fuller explanations. I hope sincerely that it will help you in your difficult task.

Of course, it is not enough for a book to be written. It has to be read, studied, learnt; so don't just keep it on your bookshelf.

London, 1985

Joy Parkinson

Preface to the first edition

Some of the material in this book was written specially for the overseas doctors working in London who attended the courses I run at the British Council. It soon became clear that the course was only coping with a tiny fraction of the doctors in this country and that a book was required to give the help needed urgently.

Most of you come to England for one of three purposes; to do research work on a specialised subject, to follow a course which in many cases will lead to a higher degree, or to work in our hospitals. In each of these cases, language plays an important part in your work but it is not until you arrive in England that you realise just how important. You may be able to read articles in medical journals with not too much difficulty but when you have to deal with the active language skills: writing and speaking, it is quite another matter.

Even before coming to England you will have to write letters. Chapter 3 provides model letters for most of the situations you are likely to have to face, and Chapter 4 gives a complete list of medical degrees and diplomas and the institutions where you can study for these.

On arrival in this country your first shock will be the vast difference between written and spoken English. There are almost two languages: book words and colloquial words. Many of you doctors will work with patients: men, women and children of all types, in our hospitals. To do this, you must understand them. To understand them you must be able to recognise the colloquial and idiomatic expressions they use. At the same time you must be able to speak to them in a simple way so that they will understand you. The chapters dealing with colloquial language, idioms and phrasal verbs will give you the various words and phrases most commonly used by doctors and patients. The case histories should serve as models of the initial questions to be asked.

There are also chapters about the structure of the National Health Service, the people you meet working in hospitals, their titles and functions and a selection of abbreviations in general use.

Whilst writing this book I have been encouraged by the response of all the British doctors with whom I came in contact. They are well aware of the tremendous linguistic difficulties the overseas doctor faces here. They assured me of the need for such a book and I sincerely hope that it will enable you to overcome some of these difficulties and make your stay in this country easier and your work more efficient.

1969   Joy Parkinson

Special note on weights and measures

Although the UK has officially adopted the metric system of weights and measures, many people still use the former system so it is important to understand both:

1 ounce (oz) = 28.35 grams
16 oz = 1 pound (lb) = 0.454 kilograms
14 lb = 1 stone (st) = 6.356 kilograms

1 inch (in) = 2.54 cm
12 in = 1 foot (ft) = 30.479 cm
3 feet = 1 yard (yd) = 0.9144 m

Temperature equivalents:
To convert degrees Fahrenheit (°F) to degrees Celsius or centigrade (°C) subtract 32 and multiply the remainder by 5/9.
98.6°F = 37°C

1 The structure of the National Health Service

On 6th November 1946 the National Health Service Act, after passing through Parliament, received the Royal Assent and was brought into operation on 5th July 1948. Since that date the people of the UK have been able to make use of one of the most elaborate, most comprehensive health services in the world. The NHS, a multi-billion pound enterprise, is the country's largest employer with about 1 200 000 workers.

The money for the NHS comes mainly from general taxation but all employed people make some contribution to the cost of the service through their weekly National Insurance payments. Most medical treatment is free but charges are made for some items including drugs, spectacles and dental care. Free emergency medical treatment is given to any visitor from abroad who becomes ill whilst in this country but those who come to England specifically for treatment must pay for it.

An interesting aspect of the NHS is that the patient can choose between NHS or private treatment at any time; moreover, he can take one part with the service, the other privately. So, he may go to a NHS doctor but to a dentist privately. If a patient is dissatisfied with his NHS family doctor or dentist, he may change to another one. In fact, more than 90% of the population use the NHS in some form. Only about 10% of hospital care is provided from the private sector.

This freedom of choice applies to doctors and dentists too. They are able to choose whether they want to join the NHS or not, and if they wish they can have NHS and private patients. In fact, the majority work in the service.

THE STRUCTURE OF THE NHS

A number of major changes in the organisation of the NHS have taken place in recent years. Following the Griffiths Report on Management (1983), a structure of general management of the NHS was introduced in 1984.

Government policy in the White Paper, 'Working for Patients', presented to Parliament in 1989, added the concept of an internal market within the NHS. Another White Paper, 'Caring for People; Community Care in the next decade and beyond', published in 1989, proposed major changes in long-term hospital care. These are being supported by Government regulation and legislation coming into effect during the 1990s.

THE PRESENT STRUCTURE

The Department of Health

The Secretary of State for Health is the head of the Department of Health (DoH). This is a political appointment. The staff of the Department of Health are civil servants. The Secretary of State is responsible to Parliament for the NHS and officers of the DoH assist him in major policy decisions.

Function

The work of the DoH is to assist the Secretary of State in the following ways:

To decide the kind, scale and balance of service to be provided in regions.

To guide and support the Regional Health Authorities and to allocate to them the necessary resources.

To provide a specialist contribution on personnel, finance, property and building supply.

To carry out some research and to prepare national statistics.

To support the Secretary of State in his Parliamentary and public duties.

Health Authorities

There are Regional Health Authorities (RHAs) and District Health Authorities (DHAs).

The RHAs have been responsible for strategic planning and for deciding priorities. They have also been responsible for the planning of new hospitals and other health buildings in the region. Proposals for the future mean that much of this work will be delegated to the DHAs — the local level.

The DHAs have the responsibility to buy health care for the people of their district, based on their assessment of the health needs of their people. They may purchase health care direct from Units, Hospitals or Community Services, directly managed by them, or from Units which have become self-governing Trusts within the NHS or from private health services.

Organisation The DHAs have a District General Manager who is personally accountable to the Authority for services provided by that Authority. Each Unit is headed by a Unit General Manager (UGM) with the same responsibility within the Unit. These managers will receive professional advice from doctors, nurses and other health workers.

Organisation of the proposed NHS Trusts will be similar from the point of view of the doctor.

Family Practitioner Services

Family doctors, dentists, pharmacists and opticians provide services to the NHS under contract with Family Practitioner Services Authorities (now replacing Family Practitioner Committees). FPSAs will have management responsibilities for administering their contracts and for providing certain support services. They will also investigate complaints by patients against contractors under the NHS (Service Committees and Tribunals) Regulations 1974.

Social services

Social services, often called community care, dealing with problems such as housing for handicapped people, domestic help for the sick and elderly, immunisation and vaccination, are planned and controlled by local government authorities. The cost of the social services comes mainly from local government funds. Although financed separately, it is very important that health and social services should be planned jointly, especially for the old, the mentally and physically handicapped and the mentally ill. Under the 1973 Act there is a statutory responsibility for all health authorities to plan with the corresponding local government authorities and this has been strengthened by recent legislation. This co-operation is vital to the success of the NHS.

Community Health Councils

The NHS Reorganisation Act 1973 set up Community Health Councils (CHCs). These CHCs represent the views of the people who use the NHS. There is one for each health district. Half of the CHC membership is appointed by local authorities: one third is nominated by voluntary organisations and the rest are chosen by the RHA. There are usually from 18 to 24 members who are unpaid but may claim expenses. They have direct access to the Minister on changes in the health services.

Function

A CHC's main task is to represent to its DHA the interests of the public in the health service in its district. It has the power to seek information, to inspect hospitals, the right to consult senior officers of the DHAs and to get information from them, and the duty to issue annual reports. It is also able to help patients with grievances.

Health Service Commissioner

Another feature of the NHS is the Health Service Commissioners (Ombudsmen) who investigate certain complaints, other than those involving clinical judgement, against NHS authorities. The Health Service has formal procedures for complaints against doctors. These procedures are operated by the General Managers of the Units in which they work. A person who wishes to complain can contact a Commissioner direct but he cannot investigate a complaint until the health authority concerned has investigated the matter. If after receiving a reply the person is still dissatisfied and the complaint is within his jurisdiction, as defined by Statute, the Commissioner may investigate it further.

2 The organisation of a hospital

The management of hospitals is organised by the Unit General Manager of the hospital concerned and is increasingly being designed on the basis that decisions and control of resources are delegated to the lowest appropriate level within the organisation. This is a prime concept in the Government's Resource Management Initiative, and is good management practice.

In many hospitals Clinical Directorates (or groups with the same function with different names) are the main unit of management which doctors will encounter. These Directorates are responsible for the care of a particular group of patients looked after by a specialty or a group of specialties. In other hospitals, this reorganisation has not gone so far and there is still a more centralised structure with assistants to the General Manager dealing with specific services, such as Inpatients or Outpatients.

In running the hospital, the General Manager will have the benefit of a team of Senior Managers with medical, nursing and other professional advice who will meet together to co-ordinate services.

THE STAFF OF A HOSPITAL

Medical staff

The range of medical posts in a hospital, from the most senior to the most junior are:
    Consultant
    Medical Assistant

Senior Registrar
Registrar
Staff Doctor
Senior House Officer
Pre-registration House Officer.

Consultant

The Consultant, the most senior grade in medical posts, has the ultimate decision on patient care. A team of doctors is known as *a firm*, meaning a unit, and one hears the expression, for example, 'I'm working on Mr Black's firm', which means in his team. A large firm may have as many as five consultants, but each one carries formal responsibility for his own patients.

A consultancy is a permanent post but it can be full time or part time, allowing a doctor to spend some time in private practice.

Part-time appointments are calculated in terms of half-day sessions of $3\frac{1}{2}$ hours. Both full and part-time consultants may work on a sessional basis at more than one hospital.

In order to be a consultant, the highest qualifications are required including, for example, the postgraduate diplomas such as FRCS for surgery, the MRCP for physicians, the higher degrees such as MD and MS and accreditation by the appropriate higher specialist training committee of one of the Royal Colleges. The male surgeons are addressed as *Mr X and the female surgeons as Miss or *Mrs Y; the other consultants as Doctor Z.

Medical Assistant

Doctors occupying these posts have many years' experience, but may not possess the appropriate qualifications to be eligible for consultant posts.

---

*Pronounced 'mister', but never written this way.
*Pronounced 'missis', but never written this way.

Senior Registrar

The Senior Registrar is a potential consultant who has worked as a Registrar for two years in his specialty in a teaching hospital after two years in a general hospital. He will have the highest degrees of his chosen specialty. As with the consultants, the surgical senior registrar would be addressed as Mr X, Miss or Mrs Y and the others as Dr Z.

Registrar

Registrars are addressed as Doctor or Mr X, Miss or Mrs Y according to whether they are medical or surgical. The Registrar will practically always have a higher qualification.

A Surgical Registrar will do the routine surgery, for example, appendicectomy, hernia etc, without the supervision of a more senior surgeon but he will only perform major operations with a more senior surgeon present.

Staff Doctor

This is a new grade introduced for those who do not wish to progress up the career ladder to the Consultant post. They will have spent a minimum of three years in the Senior House Officer grade.

Senior House Officer

The Senior House Officer will have completed the necessary qualifying period as a House Officer and will probably be studying for a higher qualification. Appointments may be for periods of 6 months upwards and such posts are frequently part of a rotating training scheme. SHOs are almost always required to be resident in the hospital when on duty. They look after the routine medical care of the patient.

Pre-registration House Officers

Since 1953 it has been compulsory for newly qualified doctors to serve one year as a pre-registration house officer before being admitted to the Register. Pre-registration posts exist in the majority of general hospitals. These doctors are considered in law to be doctors only for the purpose of a specific post. They carry heavy responsibility for the day-to-day running of many firms.

Nursing staff

Approximately 10% of nursing staff in NHS hospitals are men. The percentage is much higher in mental hospitals. It is difficult to recognise the different grades of the nursing staff of a hospital since every hospital is free to choose its own uniform. In addition, many senior nursing staff no longer wear uniform. However, although the dress worn by nursing staff differs from hospital to hospital, the grades are the same and are as follows.

Director of Nursing Services

This post carries overall responsibility for the nursing services within one or more hospitals, and for nursing administration. It may also involve a general management function.

Senior Nurse

There may be several Senior Nurses responsible to Directors of Nursing Services for the management of, for example, a small hospital, a number of wards or a specific service such as those for elderly people or the mentally ill.

Senior Clinical Nurse

She is a qualified and experienced nurse (RGN) and is in charge of a particular clinic or operating theatre. She is addressed either as Sister or by her own name. A male Senior Clinical Nurse is addressed as Mr X or Charge Nurse.

Ward Sister/Charge Nurse

She is also a fully qualified and experienced nurse (RGN) and has responsibility for organising and running a ward or department. She is addressed as Sister. A Charge Nurse is the male equivalent of a Ward Sister. He is addressed as Mr X.

Staff Nurse

He or she is accountable to the Ward Sister or Charge Nurse and is addressed as Staff Nurse or often as 'Staff'. This is the first post that nurses trained as RGNs or RMNs (see later) will hold.

State Enrolled Nurse

He or she is a qualified nurse who has completed the shorter SEN course (see later). State Enrolled Nurses cannot become Ward Sisters or Charge Nurses without obtaining an RGN qualification. The current SEN training has been discontinued.

Student Nurses

These are nurses in training.

Nursing qualifications

There are a number of nursing qualifications, but those most frequently held are:

Registered General Nurse (RGN). It usually takes three years to gain this qualification and examinations have to be passed at the end of each year. There are separate nurse trainings for registration as a general sick children's (RSCN), psychiatric (RMN) or mental handicap (RNMS) nurse.

Nursing Auxiliaries or Nursing Assistants

Most hospitals employ a number of untrained men and women as

Nursing Auxiliaries or Assistants. They assist with patient care and give a valuable service in relieving the qualified nurse of many duties.

Nursing Cadets

Many hospitals take young people as Nursing Cadets when they leave school at 16, before they start their formal training at the age of 18. Cadets work in many departments to gain wide experience, although they are not allowed to work on the wards before they are 17, nor are they allowed to work on maternity, gynaecological or terminal illness wards.

Paramedical staff

In addition to the medical and nursing staff of a hospital there are the many other people who work in the allied professions, including the following:

Chiropodists

Treatment under the NHS is mainly for the elderly.

Dietitians

Most hospitals have one or more dietitians and facilities for the preparation of special diets. The dietitian will assist the medical staff by advising their patients on diets. In many hospitals the dietitian takes part in outpatient clinics to give advice to patients referred to her by consultants.

Pharmacists

All general hospitals will employ qualified pharmacists, and other specialist hospitals like psychiatric and mental handicap probably will too.

Physiotherapists

These people are trained to give treatment by massage, exercise, hydrotherapy and electrotherapy, to help restore specific bodily functions.

Remedial Gymnasts

These are involved in rehabilitation following operations and medical accidents, such as strokes. They help patients to overcome disabilities by the use of corrective exercises.

Occupational Therapists

These are found in many general hospitals and in all specialist hospitals. They are extremely important in the work of rehabilitation by training patients in activities which help restore their mental and physical capability, and where this is not possible by assisting them overcome their handicaps by the provision of suitable aids.

Radiographers

Radiographers take X-rays and operate equipment in X-ray Departments for diagnostic purposes. Some radiographers who are specialists in radiotherapy treatment operate radiotherapy machines under the direction of radiotherapists.

Medical Laboratory Scientific Officers

These people work in departments responsible for the analysis of specimens.

Speech Therapists

Most hospitals employ at least one speech therapist who will see patients as part of their rehabilitation after strokes, etc.

Nearly all these members of hospital staff wear white coats but they frequently have labels to show their professional function. All paramedical staff except trainees must pass the appropriate professional examinations.

Social Workers

All social problems that have contributed to the patient's illness or that arise as a result of it are referred to the social workers.

The social workers spend much of their time in hospitals but since the 1974 Act they are part of the team of social workers employed by the Local Authority.

Administrative and Support Services staff

There are many other groups of staff employed within the hospital with whom the doctor will have less contact but who are equally essential to the functioning of the hospital. Amongst these are the domestic, catering and laundry staff, building and maintenance craftsmen and porters. These are often called the Support Services staff. Finally there are the administrative and clerical staff who work in a number of departments: medical records, salaries and wages, accounts, personnel and general administration.

3 Postgraduate medical training and registration

ADVISORY SERVICE

The Advice Centre was set up to deal with enquiries from overseas on postgraduate medical education in the UK.

It is essential to write to the Medical Adviser at least one year before coming to the UK in order to obtain the necessary information and to allow sufficient time for subsequent action.

Enquiries should be addressed to:

The Medical Adviser
Advice Centre
The British Council
10 Spring Gardens
London SW1A 2BN
ENGLAND

MEDICAL REGISTRATION FOR OVERSEAS-QUALIFIED DOCTORS

An overseas-qualified doctor must apply to:

The General Medical Council
(Overseas Registration Division)
153 Cleveland Street
London W1P 6DE

for registration before engaging in any professional employment in the UK. Doctors wishing to work in the UK are advised to write to the General Medical Council (GMC) many months before they intend to leave their own countries. The GMC cannot help a doctor to find employment but by granting him registration it gives him the necessary legal status for carrying out his professional duties.

There are three types of registration: full, provisional and limited.

Full registration

A doctor who holds a qualification recognised by the GMC for the purpose of full registration may apply for this. He must give documentary evidence that he has obtained certain professional experience since qualifying.

Provisional registration

A doctor who holds a qualification recognised by the GMC for full registration but who has not had the necessary professional experience may apply for provisional registration. However, the number of posts in the UK suitable for doctors with provisional registration is so limited that doctors from overseas are urged not to come at an early stage in their training but to gain the necessary professional experience first.

European Commission doctors

A national of a European Commission country who holds a recognised primary medical qualification granted in the EC is eligible for full registration in the UK provided his standard of English is satisfactory.

Limited registration

Limited registration may be granted to a doctor who holds a qualification, obtained overseas, which is accepted by the GMC for this purpose. Such registration may be held only in respect of supervised employment in approved hospitals or institutions and may be granted in relation to one particular employment or a specified range of employment. Limited registration is only granted for a period of five years.

PLAB test (Professional and Linguistic Assessments Board)

The majority of overseas doctors who wish to apply for limited registration for the first time will be required to pass the PLAB test. To be eligible to take the PLAB test, a doctor must have evidence of having satisfactorily completed an internship of 12 months' duration or an acceptable equivalent.

Doctors who intend to seek sponsorship may be eligible for exemption from taking the PLAB test (see Sponsorship, page 20).

The majority of overseas doctors, however, who wish to apply for limited registration for the first time will be required to pass the PLAB test.

The PLAB test comprises two parts: the medical and the English language.

Medical component.   This part of the test consists of four parts: (i) a Multiple Choice Question examination (MCQ), (ii) a Clinical Problem Solving examination, (iii) a Projected Material examination, (iv) part of the Oral examination.

(i) The Multiple Choice Question examination.

This is designed to test your factual medical knowledge and recall. There are 60 questions, each of five parts, to be done in the one and a half hours allotted. There are questions on medicine, surgery, obstetrics and gynaecology. The medicine questions include psychiatry, dermatology, community medicine, paediatrics, etc., so it is obviously necessary to revise these subject areas thoroughly.

(ii) The Clinical Problem Solving examination.

This paper is designed to assess your ability to apply your professional knowledge to a variety of clinical situations, to interpret symptoms, signs and investigations and to give instructions for the care and management of patients. The examination consists of three problems, all of which must be attempted. Failure to do so means loss of marks and likely failure of the test. Questions cover the main branches of medicine: medicine, surgery, obstetrics and gynaecology and related disciplines.

(iii) The Projected Material examination.

Twenty slides are projected onto a screen depicting various different clinical conditions covering medicine, surgery, obstetrics and gynaecology. The slides will include clinical photographs, investigations including X-rays and ECGs, and clinical pathological material including blood films and operation and post-mortem specimens. Each slide is shown for two minutes. You are required to answer briefly two or three written questions about each slide.

(iv) Oral examination.

This lasts 20 minutes and is conducted by two medical examiners who test your ability to communicate in spoken English and to form sensible clinical judgements. The examiners can ask you anything, medical or otherwise. The questions will range from simple personal enquiries as to why you have come to the UK to questions on medicine, surgery, obstetrics and gynaecology. You may be asked to give the exact words you would use when speaking to a patient in a clinical situation. You may also be asked questions on visual material such as X-ray films, electrocardiograms and on results of laboratory tests. Remember your ability to communicate in spoken English is vital to being employed in the UK.

English language component. This part of the test consists of three parts: (i) a Comprehension of Spoken English examination, (ii) a Written English examination, and (iii) a part of the Oral examination.

(i) The Comprehension of Spoken English examination is a listening comprehension of material recorded on tape. It lasts for 60 minutes and consists of three sections:

1. understanding the significance of stress,
2. choosing an appropriate response,
3. listening in context.

While working in hospitals in the UK, a doctor has to speak to patients, their relatives and friends, and to professional colleagues. Some of them will use colloquial language and some will have regional accents.

To many doctors arriving from overseas without any preparation for PLAB this part of the test is most worrying because it is a new approach to language testing and because they are not used to listening to different varieties of spoken English. The best way to prepare for it is to listen as much as possible to English on the radio, films and tapes and to study the books available. Although this is the part of the test most feared by overseas doctors, no-one fails PLAB as a result of poor marks in this section alone.

(ii) The Written English examination is in two sections. It lasts one hour and is to test your ability to understand written English and to test whether you can express yourself clearly in written English on general and particular subjects. It is not a test of your medical knowledge. The two sections are equally important and carry equal marks. You should allow 30 minutes for each part. Section A requires you to write an essay of about 350 words on a topic of general interest. There will be no choice of topic. The range of subjects is wide and it is advisable to have some background knowledge of English social and cultural life. In Section B you will be asked to write about 350 words about a particular situation. It may be in the form of a letter or a talk to non-medical people. There will be no choice of topic.

In this section of the PLAB test, you will be assessed on your ability to attain an acceptable level of correctness in language, including grammar, spelling and vocabulary, and on your ability to organise your ideas and express them in a logical and clear way.

From time to time the syllabus for the PLAB test may change so it is essential to get the up-to-date Advice to Candidates from the GMC. Clearly overseas doctors need to prepare for PLAB like any other examination. Far too many take the test too soon after arrival in the UK. If possible, attend a special course. Certainly you should study the books available on the subject and the very least you can do is to live in England for some time to expose yourself to the language. In this way you will save yourself the disappointment and depression that follows failing an examination.

TRAINING TO BE A SPECIALIST

A doctor who wishes to train as a specialist requires experience and instruction in his chosen subject. The training programme should be carefully planned with the help of the postgraduate Dean of any region or Clinical Tutors at District Postgraduate Centres.

HOSPITAL EMPLOYMENT

When a doctor has succeeded in passing the PLAB test or has obtained exemption from it, he may then apply for a post. Vacancies are advertised weekly in the Lancet and The British Medical Journal.

There is great competition for training posts in some specialties, especially general medicine, general surgery, paediatrics, and obstetrics and gynaecology. You should, therefore, not come to the UK unless you have sufficient money to live without working for about six months as you cannot expect to find a post immediately.

SPONSORSHIP

Attention is drawn to the possibility of receiving a sponsorship. The GMC wishes to encourage this scheme and it is recommended that you try to gain a sponsorship before coming to the UK. It is necessary to apply to the Government of the country of which you are a national. Sponsorship may be obtained either through individuals or through official bodies such as the British Council, the Association of Commonwealth Universities and the World Health Organization. Specific advice on sponsorship can be obtained from the GMC.

POSTGRADUATE COURSES

Advice about training can be obtained by writing to the Advice Centre and to the Royal Colleges listed below. It should be noted that advanced courses are for those who have had experience for a long time in a specialist field.

MEDICAL DEFENCE

Membership of a medical defence organisation is required by doctors who intend to take up clinical practice in the UK.

Membership of an organisation may be obtained by writing to: Medical Defence Union, 3 Devonshire Place, London, W1N 2EA, England.

Medical Protection Society, 50 Hallam Street, London, W1N 6DE, England.

Medical and Dental Defence Union, 144 West George Street, Glasgow, G2 2HW, Scotland.

USEFUL BOOKS AND ADDRESSES

Books

Guide to Postgraduate Degrees, Diplomas and Courses in Medicine. Available from Intelligene, Woodlands, Ford, Midlothian, EH37 5RE, Scotland.

English Tests for Doctors by Dick Alderson and Vivienne Ward. Published by Thomas Nelson and Sons Ltd.

English for Doctors and Nurses: A Grammar with Medical Examples by Joy Parkinson. Published by Thomas Nelson and Sons Ltd.

PLAB Examination with Cassette Tape. Medical component. English component by Joy Parkinson. 1988.

PLAB Practice Exams 1985 with Cassette Tape by Joy Parkinson.

PLAB Practice Exams: Medical Sections.

The above three books are available by post from PASTEST, Cranford Lodge, Bexton Road, Knutsford, Cheshire, WA16 0ED, England.

Courses

Courses preparing overseas doctors for PLAB are run by PASTEST and Southwark College, London, SE1.

Addresses

British Council, 10 Spring Gardens, London, SW1A 2BN, England.

British Medical Association, Tavistock Square, London, WC1H 9JP, England.

British Postgraduate Medical Federation, 33 Millman Street, London, WC1N 3EJ, England.

Conjoint Board (England), The Secretary of the Examining Board, Royal College of Surgeons, Lincoln's Inn Fields, London, WC2A 3PN, England.

Conjoint Board (Ireland), The Secretary, Conjoint Board (Ireland), 123 St Stephen's Green, Dublin 2, Ireland.

Conjoint Board (Scotland), The Registrar, Conjoint Board (Scotland), 18 Nicolson Street, Edinburgh, EH8 9DW, Scotland.

Council for Postgraduate Medical Education, 26 Park Crescent, London, W1N 3PB, England.

Welsh Council for Postgraduate Medical and Dental Education, Department of Postgraduate Studies, University of Wales, College of Medicine, Heath Park, Cardiff, CF4, 4XN, Wales.

Examining Board in England: The Secretary of the Examining Board, Royal College of Surgeons of England, 35–43 Lincoln's Inn Fields, London, WC2A 3PN, England.

Faculty of Anaesthetists: The Secretary, Faculty of Anaesthetists, Royal College of Surgeons, 35–43 Lincoln's Inn Fields, London, WC2A 3PN, England.

Faculty of Community Medicine: The Secretary, Faculty of Community Medicine, 4 St Andrew's Place, London, NW1 4LB, England.

Faculty of Occupational Medicine: The Secretary, Faculty of Occupational Medicine, Royal College of Physicians of London, 11 St Andrew's Place, Regent's Park, London, NW1 4LE, England.

General Medical Council:

1. The Registrar, General Medical Council (UK & EC enquiries), 44 Hallam Street, London, W1N 6AE, England.

2. The Registrar, General Medical Council (Overseas Registration Division), 153 Cleveland Street, London, W1P 6DE, England.

Health Departments:

1. England:	Department of Health and Social Security, Richmond House, 79 Whitehall, London, SW1A 2NS, England.
2. Wales:	The Health Group Secretariat, The Welsh Office, Cathays Park, Cardiff, CF1 3NQ, Wales.
3. Scotland:	Scottish Home and Health Department, St Andrew's House, Regent Road, Edinburgh, EH1 3DE, Scotland.
4. Northern Ireland:	Department of Health and Social Services, Dundonald House, Upper Newtownards Road, Belfast, BT4 3SF, Northern Ireland.

Institutes of the British Postgraduate Medical Federation

Basic Medical Sciences: The Secretary, The Institute of Basic Medical Sciences, Royal College of Surgeons of England, Lincoln's Inn Fields, London, WC2A, 3PN.

Cancer Research: The Dean, The Institute of Cancer Research, Royal Cancer Hospital, 17A Onslow Gardens, London, SW7 3AL.

Child Health: The Dean, Institute of Child Health, 30 Guilford Street, London, WC1N 1EH.

Dental Surgery: The Dean, Institute of Dental Surgery, 256 Gray's Inn Road, London, WC1X 8LD.

Dermatology: The Dean, Institute of Dermatology, St John's Hospital for Diseases of the Skin, 5 Lisle Street, Leicester Square, London, WC2H 7BJ.

Heart and Lung: National Heart and Lung Institute, Dovehouse Street, London, SW3 6LY.

Laryngology and Otology: The Dean, Institute of Laryngology and Otology, 330–332 Gray's Inn Road, London, WC1X 8EE.

Neurology: The Dean, Institute of Neurology, The National Hospital, Queen Square, London, WC1N 3BG.

Obstetrics and Gynaecology: The Dean, Institute of Obstetrics and Gynaecology, Queen Charlotte's Hospital for Women, Goldhawk Road, London, W6 0XG.

Ophthalmology: The Dean, The Institute of Ophthalmology, Judd Street, London, WC1H 9QS.

Orthopaedics: The Professor of Orthopaedics, The Institute of Orthopaedics, Royal National Orthopaedic Hospital, 45–51 Bolsover Street, London, W1P 8AQ.

Psychiatry: The Dean, Institute of Psychiatry, De Crespigny Park, Denmark Hill, London, SE5 8AF.

Urology: The Dean, Institute of Urology, 172 Shaftesbury Avenue, London, WC2H 8JE.

Liverpool School of Tropical Medicine: The Dean, Liverpool School of Tropical Medicine, Pembroke Place, Liverpool, L3 5QA, England.

London School of Hygiene and Tropical Medicine: Keppel Street, London, WC1, England.

The Advice Centre: The Medical Adviser, The Advice Centre, The British Council, 10 Spring Gardens, London, SW1A 2BN, England.

Royal College of General Practitioners: The Secretary, Royal College of General Practitioners, 14 Princes Gate, London, SW7 1PU, England.

Royal College of Obstetricians and Gynaecologists: The Secretary, Royal College of Obstetricians and Gynaecologists, 27 Sussex Place, Regent's Park, London, NW1 4RG, England.

Royal College of Pathologists: The Registrar, Royal College of Pathologists, 2 Carlton House Terrace, London, SW1Y 5AF, England.

Royal College of Physicians (Edinburgh): The Registrar, Royal College of Physicians, 9 Queen Street, Edinburgh, EH2 1JQ, Scotland.

Royal College of Physicians (London): Examinations Department, Royal College of Physicians, 11 St Andrew's Place, Regent's Park, London, NW1 4LE, England.

Royal College of Physicians (Ireland): Registrar, Royal College of Physicians, 6 Kildare Street, Dublin 2, Ireland.

Royal College of Psychiatrists: The Secretary, Royal College of Psychiatrists, 17 Belgrave Square, London, SW1X 8PG, England.

Royal College of Radiologists: The Warden, Royal College of Radiologists, 38 Portland Place, London, W1N 3DG, England.

Royal College of Surgeons (Edinburgh): Clerk to the College, Royal College of Surgeons, Nicolson Street, Edinburgh, EH8 9DW, Scotland.

Royal College of Surgeons (England): The Examinations Secretary, Royal College of Surgeons, 35–43 Lincoln's Inn Fields, London, WC2A 3PN, England.

Royal College of Surgeons (Ireland): The Examinations Secretary, Examinations Office, Royal College of Surgeons, St Stephen's Green, Dublin 2, Ireland.

Royal College of Physicians and Surgeons (Glasgow): The Registrar, Royal College of Physicians and Surgeons, 234–242, St Vincent Street, Glasgow, G2 5RJ, Scotland.

Scottish Council for Postgraduate Medical Education: The Secretary, Scottish Council for Postgraduate Medical Education, 8 Queen Street, Edinburgh, EH2 1JE, Scotland.

4 Letter writing

Letters are of two kinds: business and private. The second type is obviously easier to write but there are, nevertheless, certain basic rules to be remembered:

1. The envelope

a. It is not an English practice to put the sender's name and address on the back of the envelope. Most English people throw away envelopes as soon as letters are opened so if you want an answer, you *must* write your full address on the letter itself.

b. It is correct to address a man as, for example, Mr J Pinter. So a qualified surgeon would be addressed on the envelope as:

Mr Robert Turner FRCS

If the man has any other title, that should be used:

Dr Peter Cummings FFARCS

Sir Thomas Walker Bt MD FRCOG

c. Letters signifying civil, military or academic honours follow the name in that order.

d. When writing a business letter to a college, a company, an hotel, a newspaper, etc., the letter must be addressed to someone. You would, in fact, write to the Principal of a college, to The Secretary or Manager of a company, to The Manager or Receptionist of an hotel and to the Editor of a newspaper.

e. A married woman or a widow is normally addressed as Mrs unless she has some other title.

f. An unmarried woman is normally addressed as Miss.

g. The word Ms is often used when the marital status of a woman is not known. Some women prefer this title.

  h. The address follows the name in this order:

   (i) Number of house
   (ii) Name of street   } on same line

   (iii) Town or village
   (iv) Postal code   } on same line

   (v) County

   (vi) Country (if written from abroad), e.g.

> Dr John Turner MB CHB DPM
> 36 Pilkington Avenue
> Wakefield WF2 9DG
> West Yorkshire
> England.

As can be seen from the above examples, modern practice is to omit punctuation for the details of the name and address. On typewritten letters, indentation is no longer used.

2. The letter

  a. The sender's address is written *in full* at the top right-hand side of the paper. It is not customary to put the name there. In hospitals and other places where official writing paper is printed, the address is either on the right-hand side or in the centre.

  b. The date is written below the address: day, month, year, e.g. 23 March 1995. In private letters the date is often written, e.g. 23.3.95.

  c. In a business letter, the name and address of the receiver of the letter are written on the left-hand side, at the top.

  d. When one writes to an unknown person the letter begins, Dear Sir, or Dear Madam, if it is to a woman, e.g. the Senior Nurse of a hospital.

  c. When one has met the person or corresponded for some time, the name is used and the letter begins, e.g., Dear Dr Turner.

  f. When writing to a friend, one begins Dear John, Dear Mary or often My dear Elizabeth, to a closer friend.

  g. If the letter begins Dear Sir or Madam, the ending should be, Yours faithfully.

  h. If the letter begins, Dear Miss Steele, or some other name in a semi-business correspondence, the ending should be, Yours sincerely.

i. With best wishes, With kindest regards, or, Yours, are quite usual endings for letters to friends.

j. Phrases such as 'I remain your humble servant' and 'Yours respectfully' are no longer used. Nor is it an English practice to use very flowery, effusive language in a letter. Write clearly and simply and briefly in a business letter.

k. Each new subject or aspect of the subject should be dealt with in a separate paragraph. Paragraphs are marked by starting a little distance from the left side, or by leaving space between the paragraphs (commonly done by typists).

Here are some examples of letters which the overseas doctor may need to write. The addresses of London hospitals are correct but the names of other places in England and doctors are imaginary.

It is *important to print your name in block letters* underneath your signature as foreign names are often very difficult to read in handwriting. Also notice that the English write the numbers one and seven thus: 1, 7. Figures written in the style used in continental European countries may cause delay, and even loss, to correspondence.

1. You are writing from your own country for a place on a course in England.

Rigshospitalet
København
Denmark
3 October 1995

The Secretary
Royal College of Surgeons
Lincoln's Inn Fields
London WC2A 3PN

Dear Sir

I should be most grateful if you would send me details of the Primary Fellowship course in Surgery.

Yours faithfully
Bjørn Nielsen (Dr)

2. You are writing to an hotel in England to reserve a room.

Tokyo Medical College
53–1, Kashiwagi
Shinjuku-Ku
Tokyo
Japan
4 July 1993

The Receptionist
Ascot Hotel
11 Craven Road
London W2

Dear Madam

I should be most grateful if you would reserve me a single room (with bathroom if possible) from 9–20 October inclusive. Please confirm the booking and tell me your terms*.

Yours faithfully
Kiyoshi Suzuki (Professor)

---

*Terms means price of room and food.

3. You are writing for permission to visit a scientific department.

Department of Anaesthetics
The Middlesex Hospital
Mortimer Street
London W1
21 November 1995

Professor S Buckley FFARCS
Department of Anaesthetics
Royal College of Surgeons
Lincoln's Inn Fields
London WC2A 3PN

Dear Sir

I have been working in the above department for six months whilst on leave from my hospital in India. I should be most grateful if you would allow me to visit your department in order to see the work that is being done there. I could come at any time convenient to you.

Yours faithfully
Rao Singh (Dr)

4. You are writing to thank someone for having allowed you to visit a department.

Department of Cardiology
Guy's Hospital
London SE1
21 December 1994

Professor C Hocks
Department of Cardiology
St Thomas' Hospital
London SE1

Dear Professor Hocks

Thank you so much for allowing me to visit your department and to watch some open-heart surgery being performed. It was most interesting to me.

I wonder if you would be so kind as to send me a copy of your reprint: Hocks, C.: Open-heart surgery, Surgery, 26, 4, 1993?

Yours sincerely
Hussain Ismail (Dr)

5. You are submitting a paper for publication.

Department of Medicine
St Mary's Hospital
London W2
4 November 1993

The Editor
British Medical Journal
BMA House
Tavistock Square
WC1H 9JR

Dear Sir

I wish to submit the enclosed article for consideration for publication.

Yours faithfully
Naeem Raza (Dr)

6. You wish to take out a subscription to a journal.

Biskopshavn 17
Bergen
Norway
12 January 1992

The Subscription Manager
British Medical Journal
BMA House
Tavistock Square
WC1H 9JR

Dear Sir

I wish to take out a subscription to the British Medical Journal and enclose a cheque for the required amount. Would you please send copies to me at the above address?

Yours faithfully
Inger V Pedersen (Dr)

7. You are writing a letter of thanks to people who have entertained you in their home.

45 Grassington Avenue
Hampstead
London NW3
30 October 1995

Dear Mr and Mrs Pulter

Thank you so much for a most enjoyable evening in your home last Saturday. My wife and I appreciated your kindness very much and we look forward to welcoming you in our home when you visit Athens next Spring.

With best wishes to you both
Yours
Costas and Helen Dafnis

8. You are in general practice and are referring a patient to hospital.

Some GPs write letters as the example below. Others complete special forms provided by local hospitals. With the advent of computers and word processors, letters will become highly standardised and computerised. It is important to state the full name and sex of the patient, date of birth, address and presenting symptoms. With non-English names, it is helpful to underline the family name (surname). If the patient has been to that particular hospital before, it is useful to mention it and give the patient's hospital number if known.

47 Elm Terrace
London N14
4 December 1993

Consultant Physician
Hammersmith Hospital
Du Cane Road
London W12

Dear Dr

Re: Charles Oxley 26 3 42(m) 42 Liverpool Way N14

This man has c/o backache on and off for two years. Recently he has also complained of vague discomfort in the left side of his abdomen. This is not related to food intake. Micturition and bowels normal. OE limitation of movements of spine. Abdomen NAD. Perhaps the abdomen pain originates in the spinal column and I should appreciate your opinion of him.

Yours sincerely
Michael Apostopolous (Dr)

9. The hospital doctor must reply to the GP's letter after seeing the patient. The following information is usually included:
1. Patient's name, age, sex, address.
2. Presenting symptoms (to remind the GP, who has over 1000 patients).
3. Any further information gained from taking the case history.
4. Findings from physical examination.
5. Tests required.
6. Provisional/firm diagnosis.
7. Treatment required:
    a. none
    b. medical: drugs supplied — strength, dosage, amount
    c. hospitalisation
    d. surgical
    e. psychiatric.
8. Prognosis.
9. What information you have given patient.
10. Keep contact open and future arrangements.

Examples of letters from hospital doctors to GPs follow some of the case histories in Chapter 5, pages 111, 116, 122, 131, 136 and 145.

10. Letter from Consultant Physician to GP.

Department of Medicine
St Luke's Hospital
Cheltenham
4 May 1995

Dr R Graves
16 Fosseway
Cheltenham

Dear Doctor

Mr T Baxter 3 10 69 (m), 10 Victoria Crescent, Cheltenham

After failing to keep several follow-up appointments, your patient came to see me this week, having finished the steroids for his ileo-colonic Crohn's disease 3 weeks ago. He has regained 8.6 kg in weight and says he is now back to normal and eating well. He still gets occasional abdominal pain, and says he has had a persistent cold for the last few weeks. He is off all medication, and looking for a job after 18 months as a painter.

I could not find any significant signs on examination, apart from slight tenderness in the right lower quadrant but no mass was palpable.

His recent investigations show normal haemoglobin, with a slightly raised white count of 13.3 (10.01 neutrophils), and an ESR of 30 (1–15). His albumin has risen from the pre-treatment level of 16 to 36, and his alk. phos. has fallen from 205 to 124 (30–100). The rest of his biochemical tests are normal. The recent small bowel enema confirmed the terminal ileal disease but did not show any abnormalities higher up.

I have emphasised to him and his mother, who accompanied him, the importance of regular follow-up.

I will see him again in 2 months' time.

Yours sincerely

Henry Simmons
Consultant Physician

11. Letter from Consultant Physician to Consultant
Psychogeriatrician.

> Department of Gastroenterology
> Queen Elizabeth Hospital
> Birmingham
> 28 February 1992

Dr Kenneth Sawyers
Consultant Psychogeriatrician

Dear Kenneth

Mrs M Calthorpe 5 10 1910, 4 Judd Street, Birmingham

I should be grateful if you would arrange an appointment for the
above patient. She is shortly returning to Glasgow so I would be
grateful if you could see her fairly soon.

As you will see from her notes, she was admitted in December 1988
with small bowel obstruction, attributed to adhesions from a previous
cholecystectomy, appendicectomy and Caesarian section. At the
time of this acute illness, she was noted by her daughter and the
doctors to be confused, but this seemed to resolve as she improved.
I saw her last Spring when she had left-sided pain in the abdomen,
which was probably related to the diverticular disease we subsequently
demonstrated and this has not been a problem any more. She
returned to an independent existence in Glasgow but when she
came to visit her daughter a month ago was noted again to be
increasingly forgetful. This seemed to be worse when tired in the
evenings. She has always been an early waker at 5 am, rising at 7 30
am. She denies depression, and does not seem as concerned by her
symptoms as her daughter. She is able to read and can remember the
contents of the page when she gets to the end of it. However, she did
get the date wrong on Tuesday, 27 February when she said it was 24

February 1990. I should add that she has been on thyroxine 100 mcg for some years and that her free T_3 was checked and found to be normal recently, as was her haemoglobin, white count, urea, electrolytes, calcium and liver function tests.

I think she probably accepts that this is a manifestation of her age of 82, but the intermittent nature of her symptoms prompted me to suggest that she should consult you.

With many thanks

Yours sincerely

George Webster
Consultant Physician

APPLYING FOR A POST

The advertisements for medical posts usually tell you to send for an application form. This you complete and it is common practice to send a typed curriculum vitae in addition because there is often not enough space on the application form for all you wish to say. Some university posts demand up to eight copies of application so it is usual for them to be typed and sent with a covering letter.

All posts demand either testimonials or references. A testimonial is a certificate of character, conduct and qualifications and it is important to send *copies* of your testimonials and not the original as you may need them again. It is wise to bring testimonials (in English if possible) with you when you come to England in order to save time.

Very often, however, the name and address of two or three *referees* are asked for; that means people you have worked with in recent times who will be willing to send a confidential reference on you to the hospital if required. Having chosen the people to ask, you must have their permission to give their name *before* sending in your application.

Examples of these letters follow.

1. You are asking for an application form for a post.

5 Margery Terrace
Durham DH1 26Q
28 June 1993

The Medical Staffing Officer
St George's Hospital
London SW1

Dear Sir

I should be most grateful if you would send me an application form
for the post of Registrar in the Department of Paediatrics as advertised
in the British Medical Journal of 27th June.

Yours faithfully
N Khan (Dr)

2. You are asking for permission to use someone's name as a referee.

Department of Neurosurgery
Whittington Hospital
Highgate Hill
London N19
2 December 1992

A B Whitehouse FRCS
Department of Neurosurgery
Royal Hospital
Glasgow

Dear Mr Whitehouse

I am applying for the post of Senior Registrar at the above hospital where I have been working for the past three months. I should be most grateful if you would allow me to use your name as a referee.

Yours sincerely
Manlio Guidetti (Dr)

3. You are applying for a post in a hospital which does not supply application forms. You compose the following application (the Latin words, curriculum vitae, are used).

CURRICULUM VITAE

NAME: Surname: Khan Forename: Naeem
DATE OF BIRTH: 5th July 1960
NATIONALITY: Pakistani
MARITAL STATUS/SEX: Single/Male
PERMANENT ADDRESS: 27 St Albans Road London SW17 5TZ
Telephone: 081-734 6723
MEDICAL SCHOOL: Nishtar Medical College, Multan, Pakistan
GMC REGISTRATION: Limited Registration No. 83/0542
MPS MEMBERSHIP NO: 245065
QUALIFICATION: MB BS — June 1986

POSTS HELD:

From	To	Post	Speciality	Hospital	Consultants
8 6 86	5 12 86	HO	Paediatric Medicine	Nishtar Hospital, MULTAN	Professor of Paediatric Medicine
6 12 86	7 6 87	SHO	Paediatric Medicine	Nishtar Hospital, MULTAN	Professor of Paediatric Medicine
17 9 87	16 3 88	SHO	General Surgery	Nishtar Hospital, MULTAN	Professor of Surgery

17 3 88	28 2 89	Demonstrator Physiology	Nishtar Medical College, MULTAN	Professor of Physiology
21 7 89	31 7 89	Locum SHO Paediatrics	Brook General Hospital, London	Consultant Paediatrician
5 9 89	18 9 89	Locum SHO Paediatrics	District General Hospital, Barnsley	Consultant Paediatrician

*REFEREES:

1. Consultant Paediatrician
   Brook General Hospital
   London SE18 4LW

2. Professor of Paediatric Medicine,
   Nishtar Hospital, Multan.

EXPERIENCE: Nishtar Hospital is a 1000 bedded hospital attached to Nishtar Medical College. The Department of Paediatric Medicine consists of 60 beds including neonatology section. During my job in the paediatric unit I was responsible for emergency duties in patient care and side-room laboratory work. I learnt the routine management of common paediatric problems. I was involved in undergraduate clinical teaching. During my job in the Department of Surgery I assisted in a variety of major operations and had a chance to do minor surgical procedures.

PUBLICATIONS: I reviewed all the cases of children admitted to the unit with hepatitis and presented my findings to the Journal of the Nishtar Medical College.

FUTURE PLANS: I want to complete my requirements to be allowed to take Final Membership examinations. After my membership I will go back to Pakistan to practise in one of the Teaching Centres.

* One would normally give the names of the referees.

4. The accompanying letter, which we call a 'covering letter'.

62 Coverdale Crescent
London NW3
26 October 1993

The Medical Staffing Officer,
Whittington Hospital
Highgate Hill
London N19

Dear Sir

I wish to apply for the post of Senior Registrar in Child Psychiatry as advertised in the British Medical Journal of 23 October.

I enclose my curriculum vitae and copies of three testimonials as requested.

Yours faithfully,
Omar Massoud (Dr)

5. You have been offered a post but wish to postpone the commencement of duties.

42 Brook Lane
Leeds 4
5 March 1993

The Medical Staffing Officer
Leeds General Infirmary
Leeds 1

Dear Sir

Thank you for your letter of 3 March 93 offering me the post of Senior House Officer in Medicine from 23 March 93.

I am very pleased to accept the post but just after the interview on 1 March 93 I received a call from my family telling me that my father had died suddenly and my mother is ill. As the eldest son of the family it is necessary for me to return to Pakistan to see the situation for myself and make necessary arrangements. Would it, therefore, be possible for you to postpone the commencement of my post to 1 April 93 to allow me to travel to Karachi?

I should be most grateful if you would consider this and await your reply.

Yours faithfully
Nasir Jalil (Dr)

Are you have been offered a contract with or postpone the
payment cannot be due.

14 Brook Lane
..
..
.. March 31 19..

The Medical Staffing Officer
Local General Hospital
Leeds ..

Dear Sir,

Thank you for your letter of April 3 offering me the post of
Senior Nurse Officer advertised in the post of March 97.

I am very pleased to offer to report for and after the interview on
March 23. However, I will report to take full advantage of the
..

Yours sincerely,
Mary Jolly ..

5 Case histories

TALKING TO PATIENTS

Good communication between doctor and patient is vital. No medical terms should be used that the patient cannot understand. The instructions should be clear and simple. In the following outline of the different stages of taking a case history some examples of the kind of language used are given.

1. Greeting patient.

'Good morning, Mrs Rayner, Come and sit down.'

2. Invitation to patient to describe symptoms.

'Well now, how can I help you?'

or

'Well, Mrs Rayner, what's the trouble?'

These two openings are commonly used by some doctors. Others refer to the GP's letter and say, for example:

'Your doctor says you've been having trouble with your back. Tell me about it.'

3. Taking of history.

Examples of language used in case histories follow on pages 59–156.

4. Instructions for undressing for clinical examination.

Be specific. If you wish to do a thorough physical examination it is usual to say:

'Would you mind taking off all your clothes except your pants (for men)/ except your pants and bra (for women). Lie on the couch and cover yourself with the blanket' (or whatever your particular hospital provides).

Otherwise you might say, for example:

'Slip off your shoes and socks' (for examination of feet of men or children).

'Roll your sleeve up' (for examination of elbow or lower arm).

It is essential that you learn the names of garments worn by your patients.

5. Instructions for position on couch and during clinical examination. It is no use asking your patient to lie in the prone position. He will not generally understand this term. Say instead:

'Please lie on your tummy.'

Other examples of instructions for position are:

'Please turn over and lie on your back.'
'Roll over onto your left/right side.'
'Bend your knees.'
'Sit up.'
'Lean forward.'
'Get off the couch and stand up.'
'Walk across the room.'

During the clinical examination you may wish to examine certain parts of the body by instrument and you must prepare your patient for this. Doctors often use the words 'I'm going to/I'm just going to' to express something about to happen. Here, for example, an examination by sigmoidoscope:

'I'm just going to have a look in your back passage to make sure everything is all right. I want you to lie on your left side with your bottom right over the edge of the couch. I'm going to examine you with my finger and then with an instrument which will feel like my finger only cold. Let yourself go loose. Try and relax. This will feel cold. Take a deep breath in. This will feel rather like the last one. Breathe in again. This may make you feel as if you want to have your bowels opened, but don't worry, you won't. I'm just going to blow some air in now. Good. I've almost finished. Good.'

Notice the constant reassurance the doctor gives by the use of 'just', 'don't worry' and 'good'.

6. Instruction to dress.

Do not walk out of the room leaving your patient unsure of what to do next.

'You can get dressed now and then come out to me' is helpful. For a disabled or elderly patient who finds dressing difficult, it is kind to add: 'Don't hurry. Take your time.'

7. Information of diagnosis, treatment or further tests.

Some doctors talk to their patients while they are in the cubicle, others when the patient is dressed and comes out to the doctor. It depends on the arrangements at the particular hospital.

a. No treatment.

Sometimes it is possible for the hospital doctor to make an immediate diagnosis and reassure the patient at once:

'Well, Mrs Turner, there doesn't seem to be anything wrong with you. I'm sure this will clear up on its own but if you continue to be worried about it, go to your GP and he will arrange for you to come and see me again.'

b. Tests.

Much more often, the hospital doctor will order tests.

'Well, Miss Hartley, I can't find anything seriously wrong with you but I'd like you to have your chest X-rayed and an EEG. Go to the Appointments desk before you leave the hospital.'

Most patients want to know what the tests involve. Here is an example of the actual words you may use to a patient who has to have a brain scan:

'You will be asked to lie on a couch. The couch will move through a shallow tunnel. You will be able to see on either side and nothing will touch you. The X-ray machine is fitted inside the tunnel and it takes individual pictures of different parts of the head rather like the slices of a loaf of bread. No special preparation is needed for this procedure. The radiographer may put a headband on your head to position you but you will not feel restricted. The radiographers can see you and speak to you but they will not actually be in the same room. It will only take about fifteen minutes and you will then be able to go home.'

c. Drugs.

As it will usually be some time before the results of the tests are available, the doctor will prescribe drugs if necessary.

'I'd like you to have an X-ray of your shoulder and neck. I'll give you a prescription for some tablets to ease the pain.'

Your letter to the GP will notify him of the drugs prescribed.

d. Hospitalisation.

It is sometimes necessary to bring the patient into hospital for observation. This is particularly true of children and the elderly. Words are chosen to avoid alarming the patient and the patient's relative:

'I'd like you to come/I'd like Johnnie to come into hospital for a few days/ a week so that we can keep an eye on you/him to find out what exactly is causing this trouble.'

e. Surgery.

There are, of course, conditions which can only be dealt with by surgery:

'Well, Mr Green, you've had this trouble for months. We've tried tablets without any success so now I'm going to refer you to the surgeon to arrange for you to have an operation.'

f. Psychiatry.

There are patients who are referred to hospital by their GPs and after countless tests nothing is found to be wrong. In spite of being reassured the patients still return to the hospital complaining of the same symptoms. At some point, the physician may decide to refer a patient to a psychiatrist:

'Well, Mrs Barnes, we've done all the necessary tests and can't find anything wrong with you but I know you still feel unwell so I'm going to refer you to a psychiatrist and hope he can help you.'

g. Imparting bad news.

It is sometimes necessary to give news to the patient that is unwelcome, frightening, bad. Choice of words is important and can help reduce the shock. The phrase *I'm afraid* is commonly used to signal bad news.

'I'm afraid this is a serious condition. You'll need an operation.'
'I'm afraid your gangrenous leg hasn't responded to treatment. We shall
have to amputate it;'
'I'm afraid your mother died during the operation. Her heart wasn't
strong enough . . . . '

It is helpful to a patient if a doctor shows understanding.
'I know this is bad news for you but there is a lot we can do to help
you.'
h. Reassurance.
All patients need reassuring whether their complaint is trivial or life-
threatening. It is a complex subject and is not limited to verbal
communication. The physical presence of a doctor can reassure: his
appearance, manner, attitude and intonation all play a part. In spite
of the complexities of the subject, certain verbal patterns of
reassurance are common:

'Don't worry about this. It's quite a common condition and should clear
up in a week or so.'
'This is not a serious condition. These tablets should help.'
'The only way to treat this is by an operation. It is routine surgery and
you should be back to normal two months after the operation.'

It is important that a doctor stresses the positive aspect of a patient's
condition and that the patient realises that whatever happens he can
rely on the doctor's support. In life-threatening illnesses, the
reassurance the doctor can give is to be near in times of crisis:

'You will no doubt want to go home as soon as possible but we are here
to help you whenever you need us.'

It is now recognised that it is quite difficult for patients under stress
to take in a lot of information. Many hospitals, therefore, produce
information sheets and cassettes with explanations of necessary
procedures and operations. The patient can study these at home. An
example of part of a detailed leaflet explaining a barium enema is
printed here to illustrate the simplicity of the language used, avoiding
medical terms. Instructions for the time of the procedure and
preparations necessary would also be provided.

THE DEPARTMENT OF IMAGING
Whittington Hospital
Highgate Hill
London N19 5NF

Barium enema information sheet

What is a barium enema?

A barium enema is an investigation designed to look at the inside lining of the bowel. In order for this to be successful it is essential that the bowel is clean and this is why you will be required to restrict the solid food which you eat and to take a strong laxative to cleanse the bowel. Full details of what you must do are given on the instruction sheet.

What will I have to do?

A barium enema is an investigation performed in the X-Ray Department. Patients are asked to lie on a special couch and a small soft tube is inserted into the back passage by a doctor or nurse. The bowel is partially filled with a white liquid (barium) and then a small amount of air is introduced so that the bowel can be seen more clearly. The doctor will stay with you at all times during this stage of the procedure and will monitor the progress of the examination. A number of X-ray films are then taken with you lying in different positions.

Is the procedure painful?

Most barium enema investigations are not painful but obviously they are not a very pleasant procedure. When the barium liquid and air are introduced into the bowel you may feel the urge to go to the toilet. We would ask you to try and hold on to the barium and air and we will take the necessary pictures as quickly as possible. The radiologist may want to give you a little injection of a drug to relax the bowel muscle. This can make the procedure more comfortable and will not produce any tendency to cause the barium to leak away.

Will I need an injection?

In some cases the doctor may feel that an injection of a drug called Buscopan may improve the quality of your examination and make it more comfortable for you. This relaxes the bowel, but also has a tendency to relax the eye muscle. This may mean that the focusing of your eyes is not as sharp as you are used to, but it will return to normal within one to two hours and therefore you should not drive for at least two hours following the injection.

You must notify the doctor if you suffer from a condition called glaucoma, have severe heart trouble or in the case of male patients have difficulty in passing your water.

How long does the barium enema examination take?

The length of the actual procedure varies from patient to patient but on average it should take approximately 30 to 45 minutes. Your actual visit to the department will take longer than this because you will need to visit the lavatory prior to and after the study and you should allow either the morning or the afternoon depending on the time of your appointment.

What should I do after the procedure?

After a barium enema examination your stools will appear white and may be harder than normal. In order to avoid a constipating effect it is advisable to drink plenty of fluid and to eat foods such as fruit that will help to clear the bowel, unless your doctor has specifically told you to avoid this.

Please inform the X-Ray Department if there is any possibility that:
   a. You may be pregnant.
   b. You are diabetic.
   c. You suffer from glaucoma.

The following case histories are nearly all actual ones but, for reasons of confidentiality, the names of the patients have been omitted or changed. The histories come from various branches of medicine so that the kind of language used by doctors and patients can be studied. Notice the simple language used by the doctor and the avoidance of medical terminology. Patients and doctors often use colloquial expressions and explanations of these are given. Some case histories are followed by the detailed language of the clinical examination, some by the notes on the patient's hospital record card and others by the details of the follow-up clinic. There are also several letters to GPs. Abbreviations used will be found in full in Chapter 6. Case histories 1–22 are recorded on cassettes and are available from Tutor Tape Co. Ltd., First Floor Suites 13/4, London House, 68 Upper Richmond Road, London, SW15 2RP.

CASE HISTORIES

1. WOMAN, AGED 29

Doctor:	I see from your notes you were in hospital 10 years ago with thyroid trouble.[1]
Patient:	Yes, that's right. And now I've got stomach trouble and my doctor sent me here.
Doctor:	What has actually been happening since the thyroid trouble?
Patient:	All sorts of things. I've been feeling very depressed for a year.
Doctor:	Did you go to your doctor?
Patient:	Yes, when it got bad. He gave me some Valium tablets to slow me down but they slowed me to a halt.[2] I didn't do anything but sleep.
Doctor:	Did they affect you in any other way?
Patient:	Yes, I got indigestion.
Doctor:	Did he give you anything for that?
Patient:	Yes, he gave me some medicine and then it was all right.
Doctor:	How does the indigestion affect you?
Patient:	All the food stays up here (indicating chest).
Doctor:	When do you get it?
Patient:	Two to three hours after food.
Doctor:	What is it like? A pain?
Patient:	Yes, a pain.
Doctor:	What kind? Burning, stabbing?[3]
Patient:	It feels like some wind there and I want to get rid of it.[4]
Doctor:	Do you belch?[5]
Patient:	Not much.
Doctor:	Does it bother you at night?[6]
Patient:	No.
Doctor:	It comes on when you are hungry?[7]
Patient:	Yes, I have a terrible pain in my stomach and I feel I'll collapse if I don't eat straight away.[8]
Doctor:	How is your appetite?
Patient:	Very poor.
Doctor:	Did you always have a bad one?
Patient:	No, it started to deteriorate 10 years ago.[9]

Doctor: Has it changed much in the last few months?

Patient: I think the medicine must push the food down and then I feel hungry.

Doctor: What about your weight?

Patient: I'm losing weight.

Doctor: How much do you weigh now?

Patient: 8 st 1 lb.[10]

Doctor: And how much did you weigh a year ago?

Patient: 9 st.[11]

Doctor: What about your bowels?

Patient: Terrible.[12]

Doctor: In what way?

Patient: I'm constipated.

Doctor: How often do you have them opened?

Patient: Only when I take medicine.[13]

Doctor: Every day?

Patient: No, every other day.

Doctor: Does warm weather affect you?

Patient: No, I prefer warm weather. I sweat less.

Doctor: Do you always sweat?

Patient: Yes, but more recently.

Doctor: All over your body?

Patient: Yes, all over.

Doctor: Do you feel depressed, nervous, edgy,[14] irritable?

Patient: I was worse before I got my job.

Doctor: When did you start that?

Patient: A month ago.

Doctor: Have you been fidgety,[15] have your hands been shaky?

Patient: When I was coming here.

Doctor: At times of stress?

Patient: Yes. And when something riles[16] me.

Doctor: Any trouble with your eyes?

Patient: No.

Doctor: Periods[17] regular?

Patient: Every month since I had my baby.

Doctor: When was that?

Patient: Five years ago.

Doctor: Do you feel restless?

Patient: I couldn't concentrate till I got my job but now I have to.

Doctor: Is there anything else you've noticed?

Patient: No.

Doctor: Has anyone in your family had thyroid trouble?

Patient: No. I have one sister and two brothers.

Doctor: Are they well?

Patient: Yes.

Clinical notes

Woman 29 years
Overactive thyroid 10 years ago
Stomach trouble
Depressed 1 yr Valium. Sleepy
Dyspepsia 2/3 hrs after food.

Appetite	Poor	
Wt 1995	9 st 0 lb	
1996	8 st 1 lb	
Bowels	Constipated	
Periods	Regular	1 son (5)
Family	1S+2B	A & W
	Parents	A & W

O/E
Rather staring eyes
EOM Full
No lid lag or retraction
Thyroid palpable
® lobe enlarged 3 × 4 cm
No bruit
No tremor
Warm dry hands

CVS	P	72 reg
	Ht	not enlarged
	Ht sounds	√
	BP	$\frac{120}{80}$

RS	√
AS	√
CNS	Reflexes not exaggerated
	Plantar ↓ ↓

Investigations

TSH

Hb

WBC

ESR

Ba meal

C.XR

Neck XR

Δ ? Peptic ulcer

? Thyrotoxicosis

? Anxiety state

Explanations

1. *trouble*: this word is widely used. Here it means 'disturbance'. A doctor often begins speaking to a patient with the words, 'What's the trouble?', i.e. what is worrying you? What is wrong with you?

2. *slow me down*: calm me down.
   slowed me to a halt: slowed me down to a complete stop.

3. *what kind*? Although the patient has admitted she has a pain, the doctor has to suggest different *kinds* of pain. See pages 179–180 for the language of pain.

4. *wind*: flatulence.
   to get rid of: lose

5. *belch*: bring up wind.

6. *bother*: give you trouble, upset.

7. *It comes on when you are hungry?*: Notice this form of question. It is really a statement but in speech the rising intonation at the end shows that the speaker wishes to have confirmation of his statement so it *is* a kind of question.

8. *straight away*: immediately, at once.

9. *deteriorate*: get worse.

10. *8 st 1 lb*: eight stone and one pound. See page xv.
11. *9 st*: nine stone. The patient has lost thirteen pounds in weight which is a lot.
12. *terrible*: very bad.
13. *medicine*: laxative, aperient.
14. *edgy*: nervous, irritable.
15. *fidgety*: nervously touching and playing with things.
16. *riles*: annoys, makes me angry.
17. *periods*: menstruation.

2. WOMAN, AGED 39

Doctor: I see you've been anaemic and you had a blood test last May. Has anything else troubled you?

Patient: I've kept getting a roaring in my ears and giddiness.[1]

Doctor: Anything else?

Patient: Yes, I am breathless.

Doctor: All the time?

Patient: Most of the time.

Doctor: What do you do?[2]

Patient: I'm a cook.

Doctor: How long has all this gone on?

Patient: Say,[3] six months.

Doctor: Since your treatment with iron?[4]

Patient: Yes. I keep getting dizzy spells.[5]

Doctor: Tell me about them. How often do you get them?

Patient: They come and go but last time I fell badly.

Doctor: Does anything bring them on?

Patient: Rushing about.

Doctor: What actually happens?

Patient: I keep falling down.

Doctor: Do you know you're going to fall?

Patient: I know I'm falling but I can't stop myself.

Doctor: Do your legs give way?[6]

Patient: Yes.

Doctor: Do you fall in any particular way?[7]

Patient: I keep falling forwards.

Doctor: You've hurt yourself more than once?

Patient: Oh yes. I go giddy. The fridge comes to meet me and whizzes round.[8]

Doctor: If you stand still, do you hold on?

Patient: Yes.

Doctor: Do you feel giddy in bed?

Patient: Yes.

Doctor: Are you all right between spasms?

Patient: Yes.

Doctor: Does it affect your hearing?

Patient: I get roaring in my ears.

Doctor: What does it sound like?

Patient:	Like whooshing.[9]
Doctor:	How long?
Patient:	Minutes.
Doctor:	Do you feel sick?[10]
Patient:	Yes. First thing in the morning. Terribly.
Doctor:	Have you been sick?[11]
Patient:	Oh yes.
Doctor:	Do you suffer from headaches?
Patient:	My periods[12] are only for half a day and I get terrible headaches.
Doctor:	How often do you have your periods?
Patient:	It varies. Every two or three weeks.
Doctor:	Is it always like that?
Patient:	Yes.
Doctor:	When did they start?
Patient:	When I was eleven. Then nine years ago they stopped for three years. I saw[13] five days before that.
Doctor:	You say you are breathless?
Patient:	Yes. I get puffed[14] if I go upstairs.
Doctor:	Do you suffer from indigestion?
Patient:	No.
Doctor:	Bowel trouble?
Patient:	No.
Doctor:	Water?
Patient:	No.
Doctor:	Do you get up at night?
Patient:	No.
Doctor:	How's your appetite?
Patient:	Fair.
Doctor:	Do you smoke?
Patient:	Fifteen to twenty a day.
Doctor:	Do you drink?
Patient:	Not a lot.

During the clinical examination the doctor made the following remarks:

Doctor:	Can I have your arm? I'll take your blood pressure. Apart from iron tablets, are you taking anything else?

Patient: Yes. For sleeping.

Doctor: Let me look at your chest for a moment. Take a big breath. What are these pale patches on your cheeks?

Patient: They come from taking sleeping pills.

Doctor: Breathe through your mouth. When did you have your teeth out.

Patient: Four years ago.

Doctor: Let your shoulders go loose. Have your motions changed in colour?

Patient: Yes. They are very dark. The iron tablets give me diarrhoea.

Doctor: I'll look at your eyes now. Look at my finger. Keep your head still and follow it with your eyes. Open your mouth. Can you feel this pin?

I can't find any serious cause for anaemia. I'd like you to have your chest X-rayed, a skull X-ray, an EEG and some further blood tests.

Explanations

1. *roaring*: a loud noise.
   giddiness: vertigo.
2. *what do you do?*: what is your job?
3. *say*: about, roughly.
4. The doctor is seeking confirmation and expects the answer 'yes'.
5. *dizzy spells*: periods of vertigo.
6. *give way*: collapse.
7. *any particular way*: in a certain direction.
8. *the fridge . . . whizzes round*: she has the impression the refrigerator is moving towards her and moving round rapidly.
9. *whooshing*: the sound of a heavy volume of water like a waterfall.
10. *feel sick*: nausea.
11. *been sick*: vomited.
12. *periods*: menstruation.
13. *I saw*: I menstruated.
14. *puffed*: out of breath, breathless.

3. WOMAN, AGED 35

Doctor: I see from notes you came to us a year ago with an overactive thyroid gland.

Patient: Yes, and I had a miscarriage[1] in May and I'm now pregnant again.

Doctor: When is your baby due?

Patient: Roughly[2] 10th July.

Doctor: Have you been taking pills[3] for your gland?

Patient: I stopped taking them about six months ago.

Doctor: How are you at the moment?

Patient: I keep feeling queer and my doctor suggested I had a check-up.[4]

Doctor: Tell me what symptoms you have. Do you ever faint?[5]

Patient: No, but I feel faint. I feel hot and weak when I'm travelling.

Doctor: Do you actually flush[6] or sweat?

Patient: No. Not as before.

Doctor: Any other symptoms? Have you been gaining weight?

Patient: Yes, I didn't realise I was pregnant.

Doctor: How is your appetite?

Patient: Good.

Doctor: Are your bowels regular?

Patient: Yes.

Doctor: Do you go more than once a day?

Patient: No.

Doctor: They are quite well-formed, are they?

Patient: Yes.

Doctor: How are your nerves? Are you jittery, fidgety?[7]

Patient: No.

Doctor: Do the family get on your nerves?[8]

Patient: Not now.

Doctor: Were your eyes always prominent?

Patient: Yes.

Doctor: Are you particularly bothered by the weather?[9]

Patient: No. I used to be before.

Doctor: You suffer from palpitations?[10]

Patient: Yes, but I've had them since I was a child.

Doctor: In yourself, you feel different?
Patient: Oh, yes.

Clinical notes

Woman 35
Pregnant   EDD 10 7 93
Well but occ. c/o faintness
Bowels 1/day
Not nervous or jittery
No fidgets or shaking
No eye symptoms
Can tolerate heat better
Always had palpitations
O/E
Healthy woman
CVS   P 88 — regular
             Ht not enlarged
             Ht sounds √
             BP $\frac{120}{70}$
             Chest √
AS   near full term uterus. Tongue pale and depapillated.
             Neck — soft and slightly enlarged thyroid.
             No bruit. No tremor.
             Hands warm and dry
CNS   Reflexes √
             No eye signs
△ Euthyroid
? Anaemic

Explanations

1. *miscarriage*: natural, spontaneous abortion.
2. *roughly*: about.
3. *pills*: drugs in tablet form.

4. *queer*: unwell.
   check-up: medical examination.
5. *faint*: syncope.
6. *flush*: temporary reddening of the face.
7. *jittery*: nervous.
   fidgety: nervously touching and playing with things.
8. *get on your nerves*: irritate you.
9. *bothered*: upset, troubled.
10. notice the statement-question form (see Case History 1, note 7).

4. WOMAN, AGED 72

Woman complained of tightness in abdomen associated with belching wind which did not relieve feeling. Symptoms usually began between 5 and 6 p.m. lasting several hours. Relieved by white mixture.

Doctor: Does the pain come on in the night?[1]

Patient: Not often.

Doctor: When it comes on, do you get up?

Patient: Yes, I get up and walk round and it relieves it.

Doctor: Does anything but the white mixture help it?

Patient: I've been on a strict diet for six months. I never touch milk.[2]

Doctor: Does any position help you?

Patient: No, It comes on after tea, about five. I have my main meal midday.

Doctor: Have you been sick?[3]

Patient: Only at the beginning. I was very sick then.

Doctor: Do you feel sick?[4]

Patient: Yes, I feel sick but I can't be sick.

Doctor: Does the pain go through to the back?

Patient: No, but it goes under my armpits.

Doctor: What's your weight been doing?

Patient: I've lost $1\frac{1}{2}$ stone[5] but I've been on a fat-free diet for six months.

Doctor: What's your appetite like?

Patient: Poor as ever.

Doctor: What about your bowels?

Patient: I go twice a day, in the morning.

Doctor: Is this a life-long habit?

Patient: Yes.

Doctor: What do the motions[6] look like? Well-formed, firm?

Patient: Yes.

Doctor: What about the colour? Has it changed?

Patient: No.

Doctor: Are they dark?

Patient: Yes.

Doctor: Any sign of blood?

Patient: No.

Doctor:	Do they float on the water when you flush the lavatory?[7]
Patient:	No.
Doctor:	Have you noticed an unpleasant smell?
Patient:	No.
Doctor:	Have you noticed any difference in your water?[8]
Patient:	No.
Doctor:	Do you have to get up in the night?
Patient:	Once.
Doctor:	Your water hasn't been darker?
Patient:	No.
Doctor:	Do you smoke?
Patient:	10 a day.
Doctor:	Do you drink?
Patient:	Not much.
Doctor:	Have you any other trouble?
Patient:	No, my angina's been very good.[9] I've not had much trouble with that for two years.
Doctor:	You've also had trouble with your leg?
Patient:	Yes, they thought it was thrombosis.
Doctor:	When did you first start with your tummy trouble?[10]
Patient:	About 14 years ago.
Doctor:	The same, but more bothersome now?[11]
Patient:	Yes, it's tighter.
Doctor:	Have you ever been jaundiced?
Patient:	No.
Doctor:	Is your tummy swollen when you feel like this?
Patient:	It feels as though I'm going to burst.
Doctor:	Well, I'd like to have a look at you. Will you get undressed and lie on the couch please?

Clinical examination

During the examination the doctor asked the following questions:

Doctor:	Do you suffer from heartburn?[12]
Patient:	No.
Doctor:	Have you had any children?
Patient:	No.

Doctor:	Are your hands always cold and red?
Patient:	Yes. A lovely colour in the winter![13]
Doctor:	Just hold your breath for a moment. Breathe through your mouth. Show me where you get this pain. Your age?
Patient:	72.
Doctor:	Your periods finished when?
Patient:	When I was about 52 or 3.
Doctor:	Any tenderness here?
Patient:	It's a bit sore[14] but not a lot.
Doctor:	Does it catch you at all when you breathe?
Patient:	No.
Doctor:	Have you any pains in your legs?
Patient:	I get cramp[15] a bit when I'm in bed.
Doctor:	More in one leg than the other?
Patient:	I get it in my right leg; that's my varicose leg.
Doctor:	Apart from this, you've had no other serious illness in the last 14 years?
Patient:	No.
Doctor:	I'm going to take a drop of your blood[16] and I'd like you to have a stomach X-ray. You'll have to come specially, don't eat anything before and drink a white paste which outlines your stomach and we'll take some pictures.[17]

Explanations

1. *come on*: start.
2. *touch*: drink.
3. *been sick*: vomited.
4. *feel sick*: nausea.
5. *$1\frac{1}{2}$ stone*: See page xv.
6. *motions*: stools.
7. *flush the lavatory*: cleanse the lavatory by a flow of water.
8. *water*: urine.
9. *angina*: angina pectoris is generally referred to as 'angina' and should not be confused with Vincent's angina (a throat condition).

10. *tummy*: stomach.
11. *bothersome*: causing trouble.
12. *heartburn*: burning sensation behind the sternum.
13. *A lovely colour*: An ironical remark. She means they are a deep red in winter.
14. *sore*: tender.
15. *cramp*: muscle contraction.
16. *a drop of your blood*: notice how the doctor uses 'a drop of blood' instead of 'some' to minimise the amount, and therefore make the patient feel less worried.
17. *pictures*: this is a simple description of a barium meal.

5. WOMAN, AGED 59

Doctor: I see you have had several attacks of influenza. Anything else?

Patient: I've had dizziness and I've been sick.[1]

Doctor: When did this start?

Patient: Two months ago.

Doctor: How often are the attacks?

Patient: Nearly every day.

Doctor: How long do they last?

Patient: Some last all day, some a couple of hours.

Doctor: Does anything bring on these attacks?

Patient: No.

Doctor: Will you describe one of these attacks?

Patient: It starts with a headache — a throbbing headache. My eyes start running. I can't touch them, they are so sore.[2] And then the whole house goes round. Then it goes dark.

Doctor: Do you see flashing lights?

Patient: No.

Doctor: When you say you go dizzy, what do you mean?[3]

Patient: I feel I'll fall over and the room spins[4] round. If I go to bed, the bed goes round.

Doctor: When you move, do you stagger?[5]

Patient: I'm too scared to move.[6]

Doctor: Have you noticed anything else?

Patient: I cough a lot.

Doctor: Do you bring anything up?[7]

Patient: No.

Doctor: Is your hearing affected? Do you have buzzing[8] or ringing noises?

Patient: Yes.

Doctor: In both ears?

Patient: Yes.

Doctor: When you go to bed, do you sleep?

Patient: I just lie and it goes off[9] within a few hours.

Doctor: Have you ever woken up like this?

Patient: No. It is always in the day.

Doctor: Does movement of the head cause it?
Patient: No.
Doctor: If you suddenly get up out of a chair does it start?
Patient: No.
Doctor: How long have you been diabetic?
Patient: Four years.
Doctor: Any other serious illness?
Patient: I had my gall bladder removed.
Doctor: Anything else?
Patient: I had VD nine years ago. I was in hospital for three weeks and had a course of injections.

Clinical examination

The doctor gave the following instructions during the examination:
Doctor: Take a deep breath in and hold your breath. Close your eyes gently. Not too tight. Look up to the ceiling. Hold your arms out. Are your bowels all right?
Patient: Yes.
Doctor: No trouble with your water?
Patient: No.
Doctor: Your periods finished some years ago?
Patient: Yes. Four years ago.
Doctor: Well, there doesn't seem anything seriously wrong with you. I'd like you to have some X-rays though and a blood test.

Explanations

1. *dizziness*: vertigo.
   been sick: vomited.
2. *my eyes start running*: watering.
   sore: tender, irritating.
3. *dizzy*: vertigo.
4. *spins*: moves round, rotates.
5. *stagger*: move unsteadily.
6. *scared*: frightened.

7. *bring anything up*: bring up sputum, expectorate.
8. *buzzing*: like the sound made by insects.
9. *goes off*: stops.

6. WOMAN, AGED 21

Doctor: What took you to see your GP?

Patient: People noticed I'd got a double ridge on my neck. My optician thought it was due to nerves. (The patient had an obvious swelling in the neck.)

Doctor: Had you been aware of it yourself?[1]

Patient: No. It doesn't hurt.[2] Somebody told me I had it.

Doctor: How long have you had it?

Patient: About a year.

Doctor: Has it changed since a year ago?

Patient: No.

Doctor: It doesn't bother[3] you in any way?

Patient: No.

Doctor: What is it that made you go to a doctor?

Patient: Someone in the office thought it might be goitre. I went for a check-up as I'm planning to go abroad.

Doctor: Had your doctor ever looked at your neck before?

Patient: No.

Doctor: What has your health been like?

Patient: My nails have been terrible. I'm very highly strung[4] and bite my nails terribly. My temper is getting worse.

Doctor: Anything else apart from your nerves?

Patient: No.

Doctor: Your weight?[5]

Patient: I think I've lost weight.

Doctor: Your appetite? Has it changed at all?

Patient: No. It's reasonable.

Doctor: How are your bowels? Regular?

Patient: No. They're either loose or constipated.

Doctor: Do you go less than once a day?

Patient: Every second day.

Doctor: Do you have difficulty in passing your motions?[6]

Patient: Yes.

Doctor: They are rather hard and dry?

Patient: Yes.

Doctor: Is your water all right?[7]

Patient: Yes.

Doctor:	Are you short of breath?
Patient:	No.
Doctor:	Do you suffer from palpitations?
Patient:	No.
Doctor:	Are your periods regular?[8]
Patient:	Every 28 days.
Doctor:	You lose for how many days?[9]
Patient:	Four.
Doctor:	Which weather do you prefer?
Patient:	Warm.
Doctor:	Do your hands shake?
Patient:	Yes, I get a bit quivery.[10]
Doctor:	Has your skin or hair altered?
Patient:	No.
Doctor:	Do you sleep well?
Patient:	No.
Doctor:	Do you smoke?
Patient:	No.
Doctor:	Do you drink?
Patient:	Not very much.
Doctor:	What is your work?
Patient:	I'm a typist in an Art College.
Doctor:	And you live at home with your family?
Patient:	Yes.
Doctor:	Have you any brothers or sisters?
Patient:	One sister. Twenty-three.
Doctor:	Has anyone had thyroid trouble in your family?
Patient:	No.
Doctor:	Are you aware of anything when you swallow?[11]
Patient:	No. But I get a lot of sore throats.

During the clinical examination the doctor gave the following instructions:

Doctor:	Can you hold your breath for a moment? Can you slip[12] this off so that I can listen to your heart? Take a deep breath in and out. Breathe through your mouth again. I'll just feel under your arm.[13] Let's have you lying flat now.[14] I'm going to listen to your tummy. Big breath in

and out. Bend your knees. Look at the ceiling. Say 'Ah'. Poke your tongue out. I'll just take a drop of blood.

The thyroid quite often enlarges in young women and may go away. I don't think yours is over-active.

Explanations

1. *aware*: did you know you had it?
2. *hurt*: cause pain.
3. *bother*: trouble.
4. *highly strung*: nervous, over-sensitive.
5. *your weight?*: Notice this statement-question form instead of the normal 'What about your weight?'
6. *motions*: stools.
7. *water*: urine.
8. *periods*: menstruation.
9. *lose*: menstruate.
10. *quivery*: trembling.
11. *are you aware*: do you notice.
12. *slip off*: remove (part of underwear).
13. *just*: notice the use of 'just' to minimise an action and reassure the patient.
14. *let's have you*: colloquial, meaning I'd like you . . .

7. MAN, AGED 59

Doctor: What brought you here?

Patient: I've just been feeling terrible. I'm busy. I'm taking tonics[1] and things. It used to come and go but now stays put. I can imagine everything. It all started nine months ago.

Doctor: When did it get to the stage when it was never any better?

Patient: A month ago. When I was on holiday I felt fine. Since I came back I felt groggy[2] again. It comes and goes.

Doctor: How do you feel when you are bad?

Patient: I sleep badly. I imagine I've got everything under the sun.[3]

Doctor: Well, what specifically do you think of?

Patient: I think of cancer. The pain doesn't stay still. It moves from top to bottom.

Doctor: Do you have pain when you are worrying?

Patient: Yes.

Doctor: Do you have it at night?

Patient: Yes. I wake up with it and can't sleep again.

Doctor: What else have you noticed?

Patient: I've lost a few pounds.[4]

Doctor: How's your appetite?

Patient: Quite good usually, but yesterday I couldn't eat a thing. When I feel really low,[5] I can't eat anything. People at work have noticed I'm not well.

Doctor: You are 59 and a commercial artist. Have you any worries?

Patient: No. The governor at times is a bit grumpy but . . .[6]

Doctor: Are you usually cheerful?

Patient: Yes.

Doctor: Have you felt low before?

Patient: Yes. I came here. I had palpitations.

Doctor: Has anything started this off?[7]

Patient: No.

Doctor: How about your water? Do you get up in the night?[8]

Patient: I get up once.

Doctor:	And your bowels?
Patient:	All right
Doctor:	Do you smoke?
Patient:	15 a day.
Doctor:	Drink?
Patient:	No.
Doctor:	Have you had any serious illnesses in the past?
Patient:	Appendicitis when I was 15.
Doctor:	Do you suffer from headaches?
Patient:	No, not normally.
Doctor:	Are you married?
Patient:	Yes.
Doctor:	Has your wife noticed any change?
Patient:	I'm depressed and tearful. Nervousness runs in the family. I've two brothers and three sisters all with nerves.

Clinical notes

O/E
Anxious

CVS	Peripheral pulses √
	P 72 reg
	BP $\frac{160}{90}$
	Ht not enlarged
Chest:	Slightly emphysematous
	No glands
Abd.	No masses
CNS	NAD
△	Anxiety — Reassured

Explanations

1. *tonics*: patent medicines, bought from chemist's shop. Widely taken by people who feel unwell but not ill enough to go to a doctor. *It:* the condition of being unwell.
2. *groggy*: unwell.

3. *everything under the sun*: every possible disease.
4. *lost a few pounds*: in weight.
5. *low*: depressed.
6. *governor*: my boss, employer.
   grumpy: bad-tempered.
7. *started this off*: caused this.
8. *get up in the night*: get out of bed to micturate.

8. MAN, AGED 35

Doctor:	Well, what is the trouble?
Patient:	I'm losing weight. I'm tired all the time.
Doctor:	How long have you noticed you were not quite well?
Patient:	A year.
Doctor:	How much weight have you lost?
Patient:	Half a stone. It fell and picked up again.[1]
Doctor:	How?
Patient:	It just happened.
Doctor:	Is there anything else you've noticed?
Patient:	No.
Doctor:	Have you a cough?
Patient:	No.
Doctor:	Any aches or pains?[2]
Patient:	No.
Doctor:	Are you short of breath?[3]
Patient:	Yes, when I play cricket.
Doctor:	Apart from games[4] — running for a bus, going upstairs?
Patient:	No.
Doctor:	How is your appetite?
Patient:	Rather poor lately?
Doctor:	How often do you open your bowels?
Patient:	Once a day.
Doctor:	They are not loose?
Patient:	No.
Doctor:	How's your water?
Patient:	All right.
Doctor:	Do you smoke?
Patient:	10 a day, but I don't seem to get much pleasure from it these days.
Doctor:	Do you drink?
Patient:	No.
Doctor:	Which weather do you prefer?
Patient:	Hot.
Doctor:	Do you sweat a lot?
Patient:	Only my fingers and feet.
Doctor:	Have you any palpitations?

Patient:	No.
Doctor:	Are you nervous, on edge?[5]
Patient:	No. I'm a placid soul.[6]
Doctor:	Are your hands shaky?[7]
Patient:	No.
Doctor:	You had jaundice in 1987 and 1992. Were you in hospital?
Patient:	No.
Doctor:	Do you know what was wrong?
Patient:	Hepatitis.
Doctor:	You were told not to drink for a year?[8]
Patient:	Yes.
Doctor:	I'll just examine you.

Clinical notes

O/E
Male 35   6 ft 6 in
Not anaemic

CVS   BP $\frac{120}{85}$

                 Heart sounds √
                 P 56 reg
Chest   √
AS   Abd. √ apart from slight
                 tenderness in R hypochondrium
△ ?   Subacute hepatitis
                 Reassure
Tests: Liver function tests

Explanations

1. *half a stone*: seven pounds, See page xv.
   fell and picked up again: my weight decreased and then increased again.
2. *aches or pains*: really the same thing. See page 179 for use.
3. *short of breath*: breathless.

4. *apart from games*: in addition to when you play games.
5. *on edge*: nervous, tense, unrelaxed.
6. *placid soul*: very calm person.
7. *shaky*: trembling.
8. *you were told* . . . this is a statement-question. The doctor makes a statement but by the intonation the patient knows he wants confirmation.

9. WOMAN, AGED 30

Doctor: Good morning. Come and sit down. Now . . . you've come for advice on family planning?

Patient: Yes, Doctor.

Doctor: Have you used any form of contraceptive before?

Patient: No, Doctor.

Doctor: What about your husband? Has he been using a sheath?

Patient: No. He didn't fancy them, but he's tried to be careful-like.[1]

Doctor: Did you go in for[2] the last two babies?

Patient: No, not really. I just seemed to fall[3] in spite of him being careful and that's why I've come to see you today.

Doctor: Right. Now tell me a bit more about yourself. Have you ever had any serious illnesses or operations?

Patient: Well, I had chicken pox and that[4] when I was little — but other than that, no.

Doctor: What about your family? Anyone with diabetes or high blood pressure?

Patient: No.

Doctor: Do you suffer from headaches?

Patient: No.

Doctor: How do you feel just before your periods?

Patient: Oh — a bit tetchy[5] but not too bad really.

Doctor: What about your legs — any nasty veins?

Patient: No.

Doctor: Ever had trouble with your legs?

Patient: No.

Doctor: Ever had yellow jaundice[6] or hay fever or asthma?

Patient: No.

Doctor: Now tell me about your periods. When was your last one?

Patient: 25th December.

Doctor: How many days do you lose?[7]

Patient: Five.

Doctor: Do you lose a lot?[8]

Patient: Well — the first two days are pretty heavy and I see clots and that, but after that they sort of ease off.[9]

Doctor:	Any pain?
Patient:	No.
Doctor:	Does anything come away from you between the periods?[10]
Patient:	No.
Doctor:	Good. Have you ever had any trouble with your womb?[11]
Patient:	No.
Doctor:	What about your sex life? Is that all right?
Patient:	Yes.
Doctor:	Right. Did you tell your husband you were coming to the clinic?
Patient:	Yes.
Doctor:	Did he have any views on the choice of contraceptives?
Patient:	No. He said to ask you.
Doctor:	Well now. There are four main forms of contraceptive. There's the sheath, the cap, the pill and the coil.[12] Your husband doesn't like the sheath, so that leaves us to think about the others.
Patient:	What's the coil then?
Doctor:	Well, this is something which is put inside the womb by a doctor and it stops you having a baby. It's not a hundred per cent reliable and not really very suitable for people with heavy periods. How do you feel about the pill?
Patient:	I don't really fancy it.
Doctor:	Well, that leaves us with the cap then.
Patient:	Yes. I'd like that.
Doctor:	Right then. Will you come and lie down on the couch. I'm just going to examine you. Open your mouth. Let me listen to your chest. Now I'm going to feel your tummy. Now I'm going to have a look at you down below.[13] Now I'm going to examine you inside. Good. Everything seems to be all right there. I'm going to put a cap in for you. Get up and go and see the nurse and she'll show you how to use the cap.
Patient:	Thank you.
Nurse:	Doctor has left the cap in. Squat down and put your finger into the front passage. Can you feel the cap?

Patient: Yes.

Nurse: Put your finger further back. Can you feel a lump that feels rather like the tip of your nose?

Patient: Yes.

Nurse: That is the neck of the womb[14] and that's the bit which must be covered by the cap. When you put in the cap, you squash it from side to side like this and then you slide it into your front passage pushing backwards.

(Nurse takes out cap and patient practises inserting it.)

Nurse: Good. Now, in addition to the cap, it is important to use a chemical which will kill the sperms. This tube of spermicidal chemical should be used every time you put the cap in. Squeeze two inches in the centre like this and then half way round the rim like this. Put your cap in every night before you go to bed and always leave it in for 10 hours after intercourse.

We will give you a cap to practise with and come and see us next week with the cap in and Doctor will examine you and see if you have managed to put it in correctly.

Clinical notes

Woman

Date of marriage:	4 12 90
Wife's date of birth:	1968
Age at 1st visit:	30
Wife's occupation:	Housewife
Husband's date of birth:	1965
Husband's occupation:	labourer

Reproductive history

Year	Duration of pregnancy	Alive now	Pregnancy and delivered
1991	40	Yes	FTND
1992	40	Yes	FTND
1994	40	Yes	FTND
1997	40	Yes	FTND

General history

Lactating now:	No
Headaches:	No
Varicose veins:	No
Thrombophlebitis:	No
Jaundice:	No
Allergy:	No
Other current illnesses:	Nil

Gynaecological history

LMP	25 12 97
Cycle	5/28
Loss	Heavy 1st two days
Dysmenorrhoea:	No
Discharge:	No
Pelvic infection:	No
Sexual difficulty:	Satisfactory sex

Initial examination

Introitus:	Normal
Vaginal walls:	Satisfactory tone
Uterus:	anteverted
Cervix:	Healthy
Adnexa:	clear
Discharge:	Nil
Breasts:	√ √
Wt:	8 st 10 lb
BP	$\frac{120}{80}$
1.1.98	Fitted DXW $77\frac{1}{2}$ OJ
	(Durex Watchspring, size $77\frac{1}{2}$
	OJ = Orthogynol jelly.)

See 8.1.98

Explanations

1. *didn't fancy*: didn't like the idea of using them.
   careful-like: *careful*: probably practised coitus interruptus. *like:* this is a common additional word amongst uneducated people who have difficulty in expressing themselves. They add the word 'like' to mean 'sort of': 'in a way'.
2. *go in for*: deliberately plan.
3. *fall*: become pregnant, an unwanted pregnancy.
4. *and that*: other minor ailments.
5. *tetchy*: irritable, bad-tempered.
6. *yellow jaundice*: Doctors may use this expression to make sure the patient understands the term jaundice.
7. *lose*: menstruate.
8. *lose a lot*: are your periods heavy.
9. *sort of ease off*: become less.
10. *anything come away*: have you a discharge or any bleeding.
11. *womb:* uterus.
12. See page 204 for full details of contraceptives. Note that to 'be on the pill' refers to the contraceptive pill.
13. *down below*: vaginal examination.
14. *neck of the womb*: cervix.

10. WOMAN, AGED 45

Doctor: Good afternoon, Mrs Wilkins. You've come to us from Dr Johnston? What took you to him?

Patient: It's my periods. They've been playing me up.[1]

Doctor: I'm sorry. In what way are they bothering you?

Patient: They're ever so heavy and I feel so queer when I'm on.[2]

Doctor: I see. Are they still regular?

Patient: Ever so regular.

Doctor: No. I mean do you still see them monthly?[3]

Patient: Yes, but they last a lot longer.

Doctor: How long?

Patient: Oh, eight or ten days.

Doctor: Do you pass clots?

Patient: Yes and it hurts. You know, Doctor, I can't go to my work while I'm like it.

Doctor: When was your last period?

Patient: Let me see. It was the week before Easter.[4] That's two weeks ago.

Doctor: Do you have any bleeding between the periods or after intercourse?

Patient: No, but I don't go with my old man any more.[5]

Doctor: Have you any children?

Patient: Yes a boy and a girl. He's aged 21 and she's at home still. She's 17.

Doctor examines patient and finds a large mass of uterine fibroids.

Doctor: Well, Mrs Wilkins, you've got some lumps of fibrous tissue on the womb[6] which are causing the bleeding. I think we should deal with them.

Patient: Oh. Is that serious?

Doctor: No. It's not but it won't get better of its own accord.[7] I'd recommend you to come in and we'll deal with the situation by operation.

Patient: Couldn't the lumps be melted away by medicine?

Doctor: Sorry. I don't think so. An operation is the only way to stop this problem.

Patient: Oh dear! It's not cancer, is it?

Doctor:	No. It's not cancer but I think you'll be a lot more comfortable without the bleeding.
Patient:	I suppose you know best but I'm frightened of hospitals.
Doctor:	I know but hospitals are useful places to turn to when you need them. You'll only be in for ten days or so and once the operation is over, you'll feel so much better. Shall I put you on the waiting list?
Patient:	I suppose so. How long will it be?
Doctor:	Hard to tell exactly, but about six weeks. Is that all right for your holidays?
Patient:	Yes. Let's get it over with before then.[8]
Doctor:	Very well, Mrs Wilkins. We'll send for you to get this fixed up. Goodbye and don't worry about hospitals.
Patient:	Goodbye, Doctor, and thanks very much.

Explanations

1. *periods*: menstruation. *playing me up*: causing me pain, trouble.
2. *I feel so queer when I'm on*: I feel so unwell when I'm menstruating.
3. *do you still see monthly*: do you have your period every 28 days.
4. *it was the week before Easter*: religious festival and a public holiday.
5. *I don't go with my old man any more*: I no longer have intercourse with my husband.
6. *womb*: uterus.
7. *It won't get better of its own accord*: it won't get better spontaneously, without treatment.
8. *let's get it over with before then*: I'd like to have the operation before my holiday.

11. WOMAN, AGED 33

Doctor: Hello, Mrs Drake. Is this your first visit to the clinic?

Patient: Yes, but I've been to my doctor and he's been over me.[1]

Doctor: I see from his letter that he's satisfied with the way things are going. Is this your first pregnancy?

Patient: Oh no. I've three at home and I've buried two as well as having two 'misses'.[2]

Doctor: I see. Were the births normal ones?

Patient: Well, the first was very difficult. They had to start me off[3] and use instruments to get him out. Eleven pounds he was. The next two were OK but I bled with the fourth and had to go in.[4]

Doctor: I see. When did you bleed? Before or after the birth?

Patient: Before and I had to have an operation.

Doctor: You mean you had a Caesar?[5]

Patient: Yes and I was ever so[6] unwell after. I went hot and cold and had shivers all over.

Doctor: How about the fifth?

Patient: Oh, he was very early and died the day he was born.

Doctor: I'm sorry. Do you mind if I write to the other hospital for details?

Patient: No, I don't mind.

Doctor: What about the other infant who died? Was this in childbirth?

Patient: No. He went sick to his chest[7] when he was six months and died of phlegm.[8]

Doctor: I'm sorry. How are the three at home?

Patient: They're noisy devils and they're running the daylights out of me.[9] Never quiet. Always shouting and pulling at things.

Doctor questions patient further and examines her.

Doctor: All's well and you're about three months on.[10] You can expect your baby in late February. I think it would be wiser to have him in hospital.

Patient: Oh, Doctor. Couldn't I have him at home? It's so difficult with the other kids.[11]

Doctor: I think you'd be much wiser to come in to us. I'm sure everything will be quite normal but you have had the trouble in the past, haven't you?

Patient: Yes, but that was four years ago.

Doctor: I still think you'd be better off in hospital and I'm certain your next child would stand a better chance as well as your being safer.

Patient: All right but can I get the welfare[12] to look after the kids?

Doctor: We'll get the social worker[13] to have a chat with you to see what can be fixed up.

Patient: Does it mean that I've got to have another Caesar?

Doctor: I doubt it but no-one can be certain at this end of pregnancy. Let's wait and see and we'll do the best thing for you and your child.

Patient: Well, I was thinking if you did, you could tie my tubes.[14]

Doctor: Certainly if you and your husband agree. We'll do a sterilisation at the same time. Otherwise, we could do it after baby's born. Will your husband agree?

Patient: He will if I tell him to.

Explanations

1. *he's been over me*: he's examined me.
2. *I've three at home . . . two 'misses'*: she has three children living, two other children died and she had two miscarriages (spontaneous abortion).
3. *to start me off*: induce labour.
   use instruments: use forceps.
4. *had to go in*: be admitted to hospital.
5. *a Caesar*: Caesarean section.
6. *ever so unwell*: very unwell.
7. *he went sick to his chest*: usually a respiratory infection.
8. *died of phlegm*: a synonym for any infection which produces a lot of sputum.
9. *they're running the daylights out of me*: exhausting me.
10. *three months on*: three months pregnant.
11. *kids*: children

12. *the welfare*: the Social Services.
13. *the social worker*: a person who helps to relieve the social problems of the patient.
14. *tie my tubes*: tubal ligation or sterilisation.

12. WOMAN, AGED 27

Psychiatric unit.

Doctor: You've been in the Medical Ward recently. How are you feeling now?

Patient: Oh, better.

Doctor: What exactly was the trouble?

Patient: I began to feel dizzy[1] and then I got palpitations and felt limp.[2] It lasted about an hour. I woke up and my legs were heavy. It has eased off a bit.[3] I only get one a week now[4] and since I left hospital I've had none for three weeks.

Doctor: When did all this start?

Patient: Last October. I went to my GP[5] and he gave me some Valium.[6] It wasn't any good. I began to lose my nerve[7] in the street. I daren't cross the road because my legs went heavy. I was working fulltime in the day and coming home and cooking dinner, cleaning and I suppose it was all too much.

Doctor: What was the dizzy feeling like?

Patient: I felt like toppling.[8]

Doctor: Did you feel unsteady or were things going round you?

Patient: I felt shifty[9] as if I was moving rather than actual things moving.

Doctor: Did things seem normal around you?

Patient: Oh yes. Only I felt shifty, trembly, unsteady.

Doctor: Did it come on first at work?

Patient: It came on first one day when I was coming home from work.

Doctor: Did it last long?

Patient: No, but I lost my nerve crossing the street.

Doctor: What happened then?

Patient: I got palpitations and these attacks. I began to go limp[10] and I went to my doctor[11] and he referred me here.

Doctor: Did you notice that any particular thing started an attack?

Patient: It was usually at night, when I was coming home from shopping or coming back from the launderette[12] or something like that.

Doctor:	How long have you been married?
Patient:	One year and four months.
Doctor:	Have you any children?
Patient:	No. I'd hoped to start a family[13] but nothing's happened. I began crying at my periods[14] and I felt disheartened.
Doctor:	Was that why you felt worse at night before going to bed?
Patient:	I don't know. I've had arthritis and working and cooking — everything's been too much for me.
Doctor:	What do you mean by palpitations?
Patient:	I feel my heart banging and I get breathless.
Doctor:	Are you puffed[15] during attacks?
Patient:	No.
Doctor:	You say your arms and legs are heavy?[16]
Patient:	Yes, I can't lift anything.
Doctor:	Have you noticed anything else?
Patient:	I have a tingling[17] sense in my muscles.
Doctor:	How long have you been out of hospital?
Patient:	Nearly three weeks.
Doctor:	Have you any idea why you haven't had these attacks?
Patient:	I've been trying to help myself. The gynaecologist gave me a temperature chart. I'm on a diet and I feel a bit more contented.
Doctor:	Do you sleep well?
Patient:	Yes.
Doctor:	How's your appetite? Good?
Patient:	Yes. I've been trying to cut down.[18]
Doctor:	What about your parents?
Patient:	My father died when I was eleven of leukaemia.
Doctor:	Do you remember much about him?
Patient:	Vaguely.[19] My Mum and Dad used to scream at each other and I had nightmares about it. My Mum's 65 now and she had an operation on her hip for arthritis. She lives in a flat with no lift so she can never go out.
Doctor:	How did you get on when you lived at home?[20]

Patient:	We used to argue when I was younger about cleaning and things.
Doctor:	Have you any brothers and sisters?
Patient:	I have two brothers and one sister.
Doctor:	Where do you come in?
Patient:	I'm the baby by five years.
Doctor:	So you weren't all that happy when you were growing up?
Patient:	No.
Doctor:	Did your mother ever remarry?
Patient:	No.
Doctor:	How did she manage?[21]
Patient:	She managed all right.
Doctor:	Did she work?
Patient:	She worked for a bit[22] but she's very independent.
Doctor:	How about school?
Patient:	I didn't like school.
Doctor:	What about work? What did you do?
Patient:	I worked in an office typing. It was all right at the beginning but I got fed up.[23]
Doctor:	So you've not been happy recently?
Patient:	No. Last year I was a clerical assistant but I had to give it up.[24]
Doctor:	What would you really like to do?
Patient:	Well, I'm very limited.
Doctor:	By what?
Patient:	By this arthritis in my arms.
Doctor:	Well, what would you like to do?
Patient:	I'd like to be on a switchboard. You see people in offices worry me. They get me down.[25]
Doctor:	In what way?
Patient:	Well, I work hard and some others do no work. It gets me down.
Doctor:	What about your husband? How old is he?
Patient:	He's six years older than me.
Doctor:	What does he do?
Patient:	He's a steel fitter in building. He's self-employed now.
Doctor:	Is that regular?

Patient:	Yes, it is now but he was out of work when we first got married.
Doctor:	How do you get on?[26]
Patient:	Oh, all right. We have our little tiffs[27] but nothing much.
Doctor:	What do you have tiffs about?
Patient:	Oh, sometimes I get tired and he says things should be done. I think he'd like everything done nicely but I get tired.
Doctor:	Does he have very high standards?
Patient:	Well, we live in a basement flat. It gets very dirty. I try to scrub the kitchen floor and clean the window and everything but it gets dirty again quickly so I get disheartened. I wrote to the housing people[28] but they asked for a doctor's letter. My doctor refused to give me a letter. We have no bath. Then I have this arm. It slows me down and then in two days' time after all the cleaning, it's dirty again. We have no cupboard space either so everything is in boxes all over the place.
Doctor:	When did you see the gynaecologist?
Patient:	Yesterday.
Doctor:	What did she say?
Patient:	She told me to carry on with the temperature chart. My husband has had a test and I'm to come back in two months.
Doctor:	Has this always been your big thing[29] to be a mother?
Patient:	Yes. You see I used to take 10 minutes to do a job but it takes me an hour now with these arms.
Doctor:	How long have you had arthritis?
Patient:	Four years.
Doctor:	Is the main trouble the tiredness in the arms?
Patient:	Yes. I want something to take my mind off myself. That's why I want a baby.
Doctor:	Why have you given up doing things? Because you are slow?
Patient:	Yes, and because I lack confidence. If I do things I think they are not good enough. I know it's the wrong attitude but I can't help it.

Doctor: Have you always lacked confidence?

Patient: No. I used to go swimming and take my clothes off. Now I want to cover up.

Doctor: Why?

Patient: My arms are not straight. I want to cover up and go into my little shell.[30]

Doctor: What do you do all day?

Patient: I tidy up, make the dinner, watch telly.[31] That's me.

Doctor: You'd feel a lot better if you did more you know. What about at night?

Patient: Well, my husband comes home tired and he doesn't want to do much. I go to bingo[32] once a week. My husband goes to a man's club once a week.

Doctor: Have you any friends?

Patient: No. I have one who's having a baby in three weeks.

Doctor: I think it's a great mistake to get out of touch with people and get so bored.

Patient: I used to enjoy visiting people but now I feel restless and want to go home.

Doctor: It is important to build up contacts and interests. There is nothing seriously wrong with your nerves. These attacks are nervous in origin but they are just attacks of anxiety. You are anxious about your illness, anxious about your house, anxious about not having a baby. Yet at the same time your life is becoming more and more restricted into a home that doesn't please you at all. You don't need any special treatment. You've already worked out[33] some of this for yourself.

Patient: Well, I was worried about myself.

Doctor: I think the most important thing is to try and deal with some of the aspects of the increasing boredom in your life.

Patient: The housing is the main thing. I've never had a decent place. At my mother's we had bugs in the bed. I've saved up money for furniture but it's so damp and cold it's no good buying new things. I sit with my dressing gown on in front of the gas fire I'm so cold.

Doctor: I'll write to your doctor and see if he'll write to the

	Town Hall. You would be more likely to get new housing on medical grounds than emotional ones. But you must try to widen your circle of friends.

Patient: (breaking down)[34] Well, I used to go to a friend but she said I must get a job or else my husband will think he's married to an invalid.[35]

Doctor: Well, sometimes friends can say things that hurt. You must have many friends. Keep the contacts open. Then you can compare what all your friends say. It is very difficult to get houses in this area I know. I'll write to your doctor to reconsider it.

Patient: Yes. My husband would like a bath when he comes home dirty from work but all he has is a little bowl. Do you think I should see this friend even if she says these things to me? Perhaps she didn't mean it like that . . .

Doctor: Yes. See your old friends and make new ones and try not to take everything to heart so much.[36] Would you like to come and talk to me again in a couple of weeks' time?

Patient: All right. Thank you Doctor.

Explanations

1. *to feel dizzy*: experience vertigo.
2. *felt limp*: felt weak.
3. *eased off*: became less frequent.
4. *one a week*: one attack of these symptoms.
5. *GP*: General Practitioner, formerly called Family Doctor. Patients are referred to hospital doctors by their GPs.
6. *Valium*: a tranquillizer.
7. *to lose my nerve*: to lose confidence.
8. *toppling*: falling over, collapsing.
9. *shifty*: unsteady (note: this is an unusual use of the word).
10. *to go limp*: to feel weak.
11. *my doctor*: my GP, the doctor I am registered with.
12. *the launderette*: a public laundry with coin-operated washing machines.
13. *to start a family*: to become pregnant.

14. *periods*: menstruation.
15. *puffed*: out of breath, breathless.
16. a statement-question, see Case History 1, note 7.
17. *tingling*: prickling, like pins and needles.
18. *to cut down*: to reduce food intake.
19. *vaguely*: not clearly.
20. *how did you get on?*: what was your relationship like?
21. *how did she manage?*: what did she live on?
22. *for a bit*: for a short time.
23. *fed up*: bored, discontented.
24. *give it up*: stop doing that job.
25. *they get me down*: they upset me.
26. *how do you get on*: what is your relationship like?
27. *a tiff*: a slight quarrel.
28. *the housing people*: the Housing Department of the Local Authority.
29. *your big thing*: the most important thing, what you want most.
30. *go into my little shell*: hide myself.
31. *telly*: television.
32. *bingo*: popular gambling game held in public rooms.
33. *worked out*: found out, realised.
34. *breaking down*: bursting into tears.
35. *invalid*: someone who is always ill.
36. *try not to take things to heart*: try not to be too hurt by people's remarks.

13. GIRL, AGED 10½

Doctor: You're Sheila and your problem is tummy aches.[1] Tell me about them.

Patient: I mostly get them in the night. Sometimes I feel sick.[2]

Doctor: How often do you get them?

Patient: Nearly every day.

Doctor: Is it a sharp pain?

Patient: Yes.

Doctor: Do you get them before you go to bed or after?

Patient: I get them mostly when I lie down.

Doctor: Do you get them just after eating?

Patient: No.

Doctor: So you get them just after you've gone to bed usually?

Patient: Yes.

Doctor: How long do they last?

Patient: Sometimes minutes, sometimes hours.

Doctor: Are you ever actually sick?[3]

Patient: Yes.

Doctor: Do you feel better or worse after being sick?[4]

Patient: Well, my tummy feels better.

Doctor: Have you ever had this pain and sickness at school?

Patient: Yes, and I was sent home.

Doctor: How long have you been having these pains?

Patient: For two months.

Doctor: How many brothers and sisters have you?

Patient: One brother.

Doctor: How old is he?

Patient: Fifteen in December.

Doctor: Does he bully[5] or tease you — or both?

Patient: He bullies me.

Doctor: Do you like school?

Patient: No, not much (hesitantly).

Doctor: What don't you like about it? The teachers, the children or the work?

Patient: Oh, I like the teachers and the work.

Doctor: So you don't like the other children?

Patient: (Pulls a face[6] but does not answer.)

Mother:	I work there serving school meals and I wonder if that had anything to do with it. At five she had terrible cramp.[7] We thought it was nerves and worry but she's been fine since. She brings up this kind of clear liquid when she's sick. Not any food.
Doctor:	Does she go pale?
Mother:	No. She just goes out of the room and it happens very quickly. Normally she's very lively.
Doctor:	What about water?[8] Has it been more frequent?
Mother:	No.
Doctor:	It doesn't hurt when she goes,[9] does it?
Mother:	Well, she's started to complain about that recently so I thought I'd better see the doctor about it.
Doctor:	Is it when you start to pass water or at the end that it hurts?
Patient:	At the end.
Doctor:	Is her water quite clear?
Mother:	Yes.
Doctor (to girl):	Would you slip off your dress and sandals and I'll just have a look at your tummy.
While examining her:	Put one finger on the spot where it hurts most. What sort of pain is it?
Patient:	Like daggers.[10] Very sharp.
Doctor:	When you get this pain what do you do?
Patient:	I sometimes lie flat.
Doctor:	What's your brother going to do when he leaves school?
Patient:	I don't know.
Doctor:	What does your daddy do?
Patient:	He's a postman.
Doctor:	He has to get up early then?[11]
Patient:	Yes.
Doctor:	Would you like to work in the Post Office when you leave school?
Patient:	No.
Doctor:	What are you best at at school?
Patient:	English and Arithmetic.

Doctor:	What is your favourite subject?
Patient:	Geography but I'm good at English.
Doctor:	Do you read much?
Patient:	Yes.
Doctor:	What kind of things do you read?
Patient:	Sometimes murder, sometimes comics[12] and sometimes fairy stories.
Doctor:	Quite a variety. Does it hurt down here?
Patient:	Only a little pain.
Doctor:	Do you get headaches with your tummy pains?
Patient:	Sometimes yes, sometimes no.
Doctor:	Leap down,[13] and get your clothes on. (sarcastically to mother) She's a real invalid.
Mother:	Not for long. She's generally a real tom-boy.[14]
Doctor:	Tell me a bit more about school. About not liking it. Has it come on in the last two months?
Patient:	Yes. (reluctantly) There's a boy who is nasty to me.
Doctor:	How? He calls you names?
Mother:	Go on. Tell Doctor about it.
Patient:	He tries to put his hand up our dresses.
Doctor:	Oh, that is very annoying. You'll be going to a new school in a year.
Patient:	(joyfully) Yes. An all girls' school.
Doctor:	Well, I can't find anything wrong with her. We'll have a blood check but I think she knows herself what is wrong. It is obviously nervous tension that is upsetting her stomach.

Girl leaves room.

Mother:	I've been so worried about her. She's an odd character.[15] She's so different in temperament from me. We are not always on the same wave-length.[16]
Doctor:	That's quite common with mothers and daughters.
Mother:	She's full of personality and very much on the ball[17] but she's an excitable child.
Doctor:	Does she get anxious over things?
Mother:	Inwardly perhaps so.
Doctor:	Had she told you about this boy?

Mother:	Oh yes. We'd had it all out.[18] But as Sheila is such a tom-boy, I decided it was six of one and half a dozen of the other.[19] I let it go. Perhaps I shouldn't have. Then one day she got really upset and went to see the headmistress. He does it to a lot of the girls but Sheila seems to mind more than they do. She doesn't like the look of the boy.
Doctor:	She is ten and a half. Does she know?[20]
Mother:	Oh yes. I've told her everything. She kept asking so many questions I had to.
Doctor:	Girls of this age get tummy pains. I expect all this will simmer[21] down. She's not a disturbed child. Good. Well then, nurse will arrange for the test and come and see me again in a week's time when we've got the result. But don't get too worried. I'm sure it will all clear up.
Mother:	Thank you, Doctor.

Explanations

1. *tummy ache*: abdominal pain.
2. *feel sick*: nausea.
3. *are you ever actually sick?*: Do you ever vomit?
4. *after being sick*: after vomiting.
5. *bully*: use his strength to frighten or hurt.
6. *pulls a face*: grimace.
7. *cramp*: abdominal pain of a colicky kind.
8. *water*: urine.
9. *when she goes*: when she passes water; micturates.
10. *daggers*: knife used as a weapon.
11. a statement-question, see Case History 1, note 7.
12. *comics*: magazines for children.
13. *leap down*: jump down.
14. *tom-boy*: girl who likes rough, noisy games.
15. *odd character*: unusual character.
16. *not always on the same wave-length*: don't always understand one another.
17. *on the ball*: alert.

18. *had it all out*: discussed it fully.
19. *six of one and half a dozen of the other*: she was as much at fault as he was.
20. *does she know?*: does she know the facts of life?
21. *simmer down*: decrease, become less.

14. MAN, AGED 52

Doctor: Well, your main trouble is shortness of breath?

Patient: Yes.

Doctor: And you cough up sputum?

Patient: I what?

Doctor: You cough up phlegm?

Patient: Yes.

Doctor: And you were a miner?

Patient: Yes, for 15 years.

Doctor: Well, how bad is the shortness of breath?

Patient: I've got about 14 steps to go up to bed and I've got to stop on the landing.[2] I haven't been able to work for two years. I'm lucky I have two sons to help me. I can't lift.

Doctor: How long has this shortness of breath bothered you?

Patient: For about $2\frac{1}{2}$ to 3 years now, Doctor.

Doctor: Do your feet ever swell?

Patient: No, but they ache.

Doctor: Is everything else all right? Digestion, bowels, water?

Patient: I've got no trouble with the toilets.[3] My water does not bother me at all. I can eat: I like two meals a day with something solid at tea-time.[4]

Doctor: Yes. And do you smoke?

Patient: Yes. I've cut myself down to between 10 and 15 a day[5] but I've started smoking a pipe and I smoke about two ounces[6] of tobacco a week.

Doctor: As well as the 10 to 15 cigarettes?

Patient: Yes. I can't smoke a pipe after I've had my dinner and that's when I go back to my cigarettes.

Doctor: Your wife's at home, is she?

Patient: Yes, with my two youngest children.

Doctor: How old are they?

Patient: Twelve and thirteen.

Doctor: There's no illness in the family, is there? No TB?

Patient: No.

Doctor: Any illness you've had in the past?

Patient: Well, I've had bronchitis a time or two, especially in the winter months.

Doctor: Well, if you can have your woollie off[7] and lie down, I'll give you a check-up.

After examining the patient:

Doctor: Well, the trouble is bronchitis and the main cause of it is smoking, of course.

Patient: Do you think so?

Doctor: I'm sure of it. Now that doesn't mean that if you stop smoking it will get all right but it does mean that if you go on smoking it will get steadily worse. If you stopped smoking I would think that with average luck you would notice some improvement.

Patient: I've noticed a big improvement since I cut the cigarettes down and went on to a pipe because I don't inhale the pipe you see.

Doctor: I know. Well, this is the main thing. Now the other thing that you can be thinking about is the question of coal dust. I can just tell looking at your X-ray film that you've been a miner, so there must be a trace of coal dust there. You are perfectly free to apply for compensation to the Pneumoconiosis Medical Panel but my guess is that you probably wouldn't be accepted.

Patient: I'm not bothered about that, doctor.

Doctor: No, but we have to talk about this. If you want to have a go[8] all you do is to go to the local Department of Employment and put in a claim.

Patient: How are my lungs, Doctor?

Doctor: Not bad at all. If you hadn't got smoker's bronchitis, I don't think this would worry you at all.

Patient: I've been troubled with bronchitis ever since I was born, you know. It was an ailment that my mother had. She died of pneumonia. I've been chesty[9] all my life but apart from the breathing side of it, my lungs aren't opening — you know what I mean?

Doctor: Well, your tubes[10] are partly filled up, that's the thing, but it's not that bad. I get lots of people here much worse than you but I realise that it does interfere with your activities.

Patient: It stops me from lifting. I lift one or two things and then I'm jiggered.[11]

Doctor: Now apart from smoking, what else can you do? You have difficulty, I expect, clearing the chest in the morning?

Patient: Yes.

Doctor: Have you one of these little pressurised inhalers?[12]

Patient: No.

Doctor: Well, one of these would clear the chest in the morning. All you do is shake it and puff. One puff is usually sufficient. You must not have more than two puffs and no more for three hours. Is that clear? These are absolutely safe if you stick to[13] that dose. This would help to clear your chest and before you go up a hill you could have a puff. I'll write to your doctor about that, shall I?

Patient: Please. Thank you, Doctor.

Explanations

1. *I what?*: the patient does not understand the word 'sputum' so the doctor repeats the question using the word 'phlegm'.
2. *landing*: flat part of a staircase.
3. *toilets*: motions, stool.
4. *something solid at tea-time*: in the North of England a substantial meal is often eaten between 5 and 6 p.m. It is called 'high tea' or 'tea'.
5. *I've cut myself down to*: I've reduced the number of cigarettes I smoke.
6. *ounces*: See page xiv.
7. *if you can have your woollie off*: if you will take your woollen pullover or cardigan off.
8. *to have a go*: to try.
9. *chesty*: had trouble with my chest, coughing.
10. *tubes*: lungs.
11. *jiggered*: exhausted, out of breath.
12. *pressurised inhaler*: salbutamol inhaler.
13. *stick to*: keep to.

Letter to GP from Consultant

Chest Hospital
Newbridge
20 March 1995

Dr Robert Walker
4 St Bede's Road
Newbridge

Dear Dr Walker

Samuel Lister (M) 2 7 1943, 32 Park Terrace Newbridge

Yes, I agree with you that the patient's trouble is smoker's bronchitis with airways obstruction. His peak expiratory flow rate is not as bad as I thought it would be, 245, but of course it is grossly reduced. The chest X-ray film shows minimal dust change which, in my opinion, is not sufficient to qualify him as a case of pneumoconiosis. There is, of course, no objection to his putting in a claim.

Mr Lister can expect slow deterioration in his breathing as long as he continues smoking. It may help him to clear his chest in the morning if he has a salbutamol inhaler. I have explained to him the correct dose is one puff, repeated if necessary, and then no more for at least three hours. Please let us know if you would like him to be seen again in the future.

Yours sincerely
John Hamilton
Consultant Physician

15. WOMAN, AGED 52

Doctor: You come from Cyprus?

Patient: Yes, but I've been in England for 23 years.

Doctor: Are you married to an Englishman?

Patient: I was, but we were divorced 15 years ago.

Doctor: Well. Tell me about your trouble.

Patient: Two hours after eating I get pain and when I bend I get it.

Doctor: Do you bring up liquid?

Patient: No.

Doctor: Do you have the taste of sour liquid in your mouth?

Patient: Yes, terrible.

Doctor: Do you ever vomit?

Patient: Not really.

Doctor: Do you belch?

Patient: A little.

Doctor: Do you have this pain every day?

Patient: No.

Doctor: Does it wake you up at night?

Patient: No.

Doctor: If you drink something hot, does it affect you?

Patient: I feel it burning as it goes down.

Doctor: Do you feel acid as well as burning?

Patient: No.

Doctor: Have you anything else that worries you?

Patient: No.

Doctor: What about your weight?

Patient: I've put on weight — four pounds.[1]

Doctor: How's your appetite?

Patient: Very good.

Doctor: Did any particular food upset you?

Patient: Yes. I was fasting[2] for three days for my religion and then I went to my sister's and had some fish and chips.

Doctor: Had you ever been upset by fried things before?

Patient: No.

Doctor: Do you regularly fast?

Patient: Twice a year for my religion.

Doctor:	Have you had similar trouble before?
Patient:	Never.
Doctor:	Have you any children?
Patient:	No.
Doctor:	How are the bowels?
Patient:	Irregular.
Doctor:	Have you ever passed blood?
Patient:	No.
Doctor:	How's the water?
Patient:	Normal.
Doctor:	Do you ever get up at night to pass water?
Patient:	No.
Doctor:	Do you still see your periods?
Patient:	No, they finished two years ago.
Doctor:	Did you ever have a discharge or bleeding between your periods?
Patient:	No.
Doctor:	Do you smoke?
Patient:	No.
Doctor:	Drink?
Patient:	Occasionally.
Doctor:	Any serious illnesses?
Patient:	I had an ectopic pregnancy fifteen years ago.
Doctor:	Has anyone in your family stomach trouble?
Patient:	No, but my mother had gallstones and had an operation here and my sister and my brother have gallstones.
Doctor:	What about your father?
Patient:	He died when I was six but I don't know why.
Doctor:	Do you work?
Patient:	I'm a dressmaker but I haven't worked for a year. I'm having a rest.
Doctor:	Do you live alone?
Patient:	Yes.
Doctor:	How can you manage to live without working?
Patient:	I have a tenant.[3]
Doctor:	Do you worry about things?
Patient:	No. I used to worry but not now. I know it's not worth it.

Doctor: I'd like to examine you. It sounds as though this is not gallstone but stomach trouble.

Clinical examination

The doctor gave the following instructions during the examination:
Take a deep breath in and out (measures chest expansion).
Breathe through your mouth (listens to breath sounds).
I'm going to shake your stomach (listens for splash).
Let me look at your ankles. Are they ever swollen? (looks for oedema).
Bend your knees (elicits knee jerks).
I'm going to tickle your feet (elicits plantar response).
I'm going to take some blood. You'll feel a jab.
I can't find anything seriously wrong with you. I think this is due to the weakness of the muscle at the lower end of your gullet[4] which is allowing acid to come back into your gullet. We'd better do an X-ray of the stomach and gallbladder as you have this tendency in your family. We'll check on the blood as well. Avoid bending. The stomach should not be empty of food for too long. Try to eat little and often. I'll give you some medicine to take after meals and some tablets to take before meals. I'll see you in three weeks when I've got the results of the X-rays and tests.

Clinical notes

O/E
CVS   P 80
       Ht not enlarged
       Ht sounds
       BP $\frac{130}{90}$
RS   NAD
Abd   Slight epigastric tenderness
       Succussion splash
CNS   NAD
       No enlarged lymph nodes
Breasts normal

Investigations

Hb
WBC
ESR
C.XR
Barium meal
Ultrasound gallbladder
△ ?   Gastro-oesophageal reflux from hiatus hernia
  ??   Gallstones

Treatment

Advice +   Mucaine p.c.
            Maxolon a.c.

Explanations

1. *four pounds*: see page xv.
2. *fasting*: going without food.
3. *a tenant*: a person who pays rent for a room.
4. *gullet*: oesophagus.

Letter to GP from Consultant

Whittington Hospital
Highgate Hill
London N19
15 February 1996

Dr Peter Owen
6 Kentish Town Road
London NW5

Dear Dr Owen

Elena Cooper (F) 4 7 44, 3 Downside Terrace NW5

Thank you for your letter about this patient. For the past five weeks she has noticed regurgitation, heartburn and belching coming on two hours after food or on bending. Hot tea burns her. She is gaining weight. Her symptoms seem to have been precipitated by a three day religious fast terminated by fish and chips! She has had milder similar symptoms in the past after large meals. There is a strong family history of gallstones in her mother, sister and brother.

On examination there were no significant abnormalities. I think this is gastro-oesophageal reflux with a possible hiatus hernia. I have ordered a barium meal and an abdominal ultrasound. I have meanwhile given her a supply of Maxolon and Mucaine until I next see her and have advised her about her eating habits.

Yours sincerely
David Layton
Consultant Physician

16. WOMEN, AGED 25

Doctor: When did the present attack begin?

Patient: It started on Christmas Eve[1] and I couldn't get the tablets. I had to keep going to the loo.[2] I only passed a small amount and it was stinging. There was a lot of blood with clots.

Doctor: Where was the pain?

Patient: Down here. (suprapubic)

Doctor: Did you have a pain in the loin?

Patient: No.

Doctor: Did you have a fever with it?

Patient: No, but I did last time.

Doctor: How long does it last?

Patient: When I get the tablets it goes in a few days.

Doctor: Do you take Septrin?

Patient: Yes, most of the time Septrin and some green medicine.[3]

Doctor: In between attacks do you have to go often to the lavatory?

Patient: Yes. I can't wait.

Doctor: How long have you had this trouble?

Patient: Since I had my children.

Doctor: How many have you?

Patient: Two: five and six. There's only 11 months between them.

Doctor: Did you have any trouble in pregnancy?

Patient: No. It's been worse since my second.

Doctor: When you cough, strain, sneeze, does your water come away from you?

Patient: Yes.

Doctor: Did you have a difficult and long labour?

Patient: No.

Doctor: Did you have a forceps delivery?

Patient: Yes.

Doctor: Do you have to get up in the night?

Patient: No.

Doctor: Can you think of anything else that brings it on?[4]

Patient: I wonder if it is the coil.[5]

Doctor: How long have you used it?

Patient: Three years. When they put it in, I had it[6] straight away after.

Doctor: Have you had it changed?

Patient: No.

Doctor: Are you under the Family Planning Clinic?

Patient: Yes.

Doctor: Why do you use the coil instead of the pill?[7]

Patient: I got migraine with the pill.

Doctor: Do you still get migraine?

Patient: Very occasionally.

Doctor: Do you think there is any connection between the attacks and intercourse?

Patient: No.

Doctor: What about your weight?

Patient: It's steady.

Doctor: Your appetite?

Patient: It's very poor. It always has been.

Doctor: Your bowels?

Patient: Regular.

Doctor: And how are your periods?

Patient: I lose four days every 28 days.

Doctor: Have you ever been anaemic?

Patient: No.

Doctor: Do you smoke?

Patient: Thirty a day.

Doctor: Do you drink?

Patient: Only at the weekends.

Doctor: Have you had any other illnesses?

Patient: No.

Doctor: Did you ever have this trouble as a child?

Patient: Yes, when I was about five. I didn't tell anybody.

Doctor: Did you wet your bed later than is normal?

Patient: No.

Doctor: Is there anyone in your family with water trouble?

Patient: Yes. My mother has it. She's been on tablets for 9 years. When she stops taking them, it comes back.

Doctor: Is there anyone else with it?

Patient:	Yes. My sister has it three or four times a year. It started after her first child.
Doctor:	Any other family?
Patient:	I have a father and brother.
Doctor:	Are they all right?
Patient:	Yes.
Doctor:	Well, we must have your kidney and bladder X-rayed. If there is nothing wrong there, we must put you on tablets. Strip down to your underpants and cover yourself with a blanket.

Clinical examination

The doctor gave the following instructions during the examination:

I'm just going to take your blood pressure.

Stare up at the ceiling. (Examines fundi with ophthalmoscope.)

I'll just feel under your arms. (Palpates for lymph nodes.)

I'm going to listen to your heart now. Take a deep breath in and out.

Breathe through your mouth. (Auscultates chest.)

Sit forward. I'm going to tap your back now. (Percussion of spine and renal areas for loin tenderness.)

I'm going to feel your neck. (Palpates for lymph nodes.)

Patient:	I had some lumps in my neck.
Doctor:	Did you have a sore throat?
Patient:	Yes.
Doctor:	Probably a little gland came up. Let's feel your tummy. (Palpates abdomen.) Lie back on my hand. Does that hurt you at the front or back? (Palpates each loin bimanually.)
Patient:	Back.
Doctor:	Now your legs. Bend your knees. (Elicits knee jerks.) I'm going to tickle your feet. (Elicits plantar response.) I want to examine your back passage.[8] Please take off your pants. Turn over and curl yourself into a ball with your bottom[9] right over the edge of the couch. This is a bit uncomfortable. Tell me if there is any tender spot. (Performs rectal examination.)

Patient: No.

Doctor: Nurse will wipe the lubricant off your bottom. I'm going to take a drop of your blood now. I can't find anything wrong in examining you but we must obviously look into this further to see if there is any cause for these repeated infections. Make an appointment for a kidney X-ray. You can get dressed now.

Clinical notes

Thin long-limbed healthy girl
Not anaemic
O/E
CVS   P 80

              Ht not enlarged

              Ht sounds √

              BP $\dfrac{130}{90}$

Fundi   0
Chest   √
No glands
Abd   Slight tenderness over sigmoid colon
No renal masses
PR   NAD
CNS   NAD

Investigations

IVP
MSU
CXR
FBC
U and E
RBS

Explanations

1. *Christmas Eve*: December 24th.
2. *had to keep going to the loo*: had to go frequently to the lavatory to pass water (but it can also mean because of diarrhoea).
3. *green medicine*: potassium citrate known as pot.cit.
4. *brings it on*: causes it.
5. *the coil*: intrauterine contraceptive device.
6. *it*: the urinary trouble.
7. *the pill*: oral contraceptive.
8. *back passage*: rectum.
9. *bottom*: buttocks.

Letter to GP from Consultant

Whittington Hospital
Highgate Hill
London N19
5 January 1993

Dr S Popplewell
10 York Rise
London N6

Dear Dr Popplewell

Pamela Harvey (F) 7 6 68, 53 Park Close N6

Thank you for referring this patient who gives an interesting history of frequent urinary infections occurring about every 4 months since marriage 6 years ago. However, there is no clear-cut relation to intercourse nor is there any other precipitating factor. Each attack seems to respond rapidly to treatment and there is nothing to suggest permanent renal damage. There is an interesting family history with her mother and sister having similar symptoms. Her mother is on long-term prophylaxis and she has relapses if she ever stops taking the tablets.

I could not find any significant signs on general and rectal examination apart from slight tenderness over the sigmoid colon. I have ordered IVP and other relevant investigations to exclude any underlying cause.

Should nothing be found, it might be advisable to treat her in the same way as her mother with long-term chemoprophylaxis.

Yours sincerely
David Layton
Consultant Physician

17. MAN, AGED 22

Patient attending follow-up clinic for result of his investigations. Two years previously in hospital for three weeks with duodenal ulcer symptoms. Difficult home background. Overweight. Bitten finger-nails. Symptoms reappeared.

Doctor:	How are you now?
Patient:	Not too good.
Doctor:	Are you still getting the pain?
Patient:	Yes.
Doctor:	Well, the X-ray doctor found irritability and distortion of the duodenum although there was no actual ulcer visible on the X-ray. This does not necessarily mean that you have no ulcer. We have to decide the best way of treating it. There are two ways: medical and surgical. In young people we try to avoid operations and we hope that medical means will help. There is no risk attached to the operation but we can't give a hundred per cent guarantee that it would relieve all your symptoms. Most patients get better after it and have no side effects. But with young people we usually persist with medical treatment. Now you did have a spell[1] in hospital and it disappeared but now it has started again. Has anyone in your family had an ulcer?
Patient:	Yes, my father had one but it cleared up.[2]
Doctor:	Well, this could be relevant as ulcers may run in families. But there isn't much you can do about that as you can't choose your parents! The other factors, of course, are smoking, worry, anxiety, irregular meals, over-tiredness, overwork and stress. These all affect an ulcer. Unfortunately you have a lot of stress and worry at home so I feel despite your being so young, putting you to bed for three weeks isn't enough. I'd like you to see Mr Oakes.[3] He has a great deal of experience with ulcers and if he feels an operation is the answer, I think we should take his advice. Now, have you managed to do anything about your smoking?
Patient:	I smoke about 50 a day.

Doctor: How often do you get the pain now?

Patient: Every day.

Doctor: Does it wake you up from sleep?

Patient: Once a week it does.

Doctor: Have you been sick?[4]

Patient: No.

Doctor: Have you lost time from work because of it?

Patient: Yes, odd days here and there.

Doctor: Well, make an appointment to see Mr Oakes and I'll write to him and to your doctor.

Patient: Thank you, Doctor.

Explanations

1. *a spell*: a period, a stay.
2. *cleared up*: got better, disappeared.
3. *Mr Oakes*: fully qualified male surgeons are addressed as Mr (pronounced Mister) whereas in other branches of medicine the title is Dr (Doctor). Female surgeons are addressed as Miss or Mrs.
4. *been sick*: vomited.

Case histories 18 – 22 come from Accident and Emergency Departments. These are the only departments of a hospital which see patients without a letter of referral from the GP.

18. MAN, AGED 28

Doctor:	Where's your injury?
Patient:	Here, my ankle.
Doctor:	How did it happen?
Patient:	I tripped over on the pavement and twisted it. It's swollen and very painful.
Doctor:	When did it happen?
Patient:	This morning.
Doctor:	I'd like you to have an X-ray and after you've had it, come back to me.

After examining the X-ray:

Doctor: Well, there's nothing broken. It's just a sprain. Nurse will put on a supporting bandage. Do exercises and have contrasting baths. Put your foot in hot and cold water alternately three or four times a day. The pain and swelling should go but if it doesn't settle down,[1] come and see us again.

Explanations

1. *Settle down*: get better.

19. MAN, AGED 52

Man with boil on back of neck.

Doctor: How long have you had this boil?

Patient: For five days.

After examining the boil:

Doctor: This needs an incision to let out the pus. For this we'd like to give you an anaesthetic so there won't be any pain. When did you have food and drink last?

Patient: Yesterday.

Doctor: Are you sure you had nothing today?

Patient: Only a cup of tea for breakfast.

Doctor: What time was that?

Patient: Three hours ago.

Doctor: Well, you'll have to wait an hour then as we can't give you an anaesthetic until four hours after you've eaten or drunk. Are you quite healthy otherwise?

Patient: Yes.

Doctor: Right. We'll attend to you in an hour's time.

20. WOMAN, AGED 32

Doctor: What happened?

Patient: I was in a fight and got my head hurt.

Doctor: When was this?

Patient: Just a while ago.

Doctor: How long ago?

Patient: Half an hour ago. Down the road. Somebody hit me.

Doctor: Tell me exactly what happened.

Patient: I was walking down the road with my friend and we came to my sister's house and it was clear that my sister was having some trouble with her husband. He told me to clear off[1] and I told him to leave my sister alone.

Doctor: What happened then?

Patient: He threw some milk bottles at me but they missed. Then he hit me with a long iron pole.

Doctor: Were you knocked out?[2]

Patient: No.

Doctor: Are you sure you remember everything that happened?

Patient: Yes.

Doctor: I want you to go for an X-ray and then come back to me. You'll need some stitches in that wound.

Explanations

1. *to clear off*: to go away (vulgar).
2. *to be knocked out*: to be made unconscious.
3. *stitch*: suture.

21. MAN, AGED 78

Doctor: Where is your injury?

Patient: My ankle and my leg.

Doctor: What happened?

Patient: I was standing on a chair and I slipped off.

Doctor: When did this happen?

Patient: Four weeks ago. I've been trying to cure myself.

Doctor: Did this happen at home?

Patient: Yes.

Doctor: Are you under a doctor?

Patient: Yes.

After examining the patient.

Doctor: I want you to keep this up at home above the level of your seat.[1] You can go to the toilet but then keep your leg up again. Have you someone to look after you?

Patient: No. I'm all alone.

Doctor: Well, we'll get you a home help.[2]

Patient: I feel better walking than sitting.

Doctor: Yes but this won't heal up if you don't get rid of some of this swelling of your ankle. When you've had your leg dressed, don't go until you've seen the social worker.

Explanations

1. *seat*: buttocks.
2. *home help*: people employed to help elderly and sick patients in their own home.

22. WOMAN, AGED 35

Doctor: What's happened?

Patient: I've just been in a road accident.

Doctor: Were you the driver or the passenger?

Patient: The driver.

Doctor: Were you thrown out of the car or did you get the steering wheel in your chest?

Patient: I wasn't thrown out but I got the steering wheel in my chest and I hit my head on the windscreen.

Doctor: Were you knocked out?[1]

Patient: I don't remember anything after the accident.

Doctor: Have you got headache or pain anywhere other than your chest?

Patient: My head aches; that's all.

Doctor: We'll send you for some X-rays and stitch[2] any wounds later.

After examining X-rays.

Doctor: You've fractured your skull. We'll have to admit you for observation. Do you want the clerk to notify any of your family?

Patient: Oh yes. Will you ring my husband at work? This is his number.

Explanations

1. *knocked out*: made unconscious.
2. *stitch*: suture.

23. MAN, AGED 73

Man complained of alternating constipation and diarrhoea with bloodstained stools and loss of weight. Examination showed a mobile mass on the left iliac fossa. Barium enema shows cancer of the pelvic colon.

Doctor: Well, Mr Longwood, you've been having trouble with your bowels for a long time. The last time you came to hospital, we did an X-ray and this showed that there is a growth[1] which is causing the bleeding.

Patient: Is it serious, Doctor?

Doctor: It will be if we leave it, so I would recommend you to have an operation to remove the growth. You will be in hospital for about two to three weeks and then we'll see you for regular check-ups.

Patient: Aren't I too old to have an operation?

Doctor: Oh no. Age is no bar[2] to surgery these days. We consider each patient individually. Some patients are young at ninety and others are old at sixty.

Patient: I won't have to have a bag,[3] will I?[4]

Doctor: Fortunately not. After the operation you should have no trouble with your bowels.

Patient: Shall I need any other kind of treatment?

Doctor: No. The operation should clear up[5] the trouble. So I'll write to your doctor and tell him we are bringing you into hospital to have an operation. I shall probably see you in the ward in about ten days' time.

Patient: Thank you, Doctor.

Explanations

1. *a growth*: a mass, cancer.
2. *age is no bar*: age is no obstacle; here the success of surgery does not depend on age.
3. *to have a bag*: a bag to empty the bowel following a colostomy.
4. *I won't . . . a bag, will I?*: Note this form of negative statement followed by a positive question tag. The patient hopes for a negative answer. He is seeking reassurance.
5. *clear up*: remedy.

Letter to GP from Consultant

Geriatric Department
Whittington Hospital
London N19
4 April 1995

Dr C Young
6 Melburn Grove
N19

Dear Dr Young

Charles Longwood (M) 1 2 1922, 24 Highgate Avenue N19

The barium enema on this patient confirmed the presence of a stenosing Ca of the pelvic colon. I have discussed him with Mr Sanderson and he will admit him in the next few days for surgery. I've told Mr Longwood that he has a growth and needs surgery and that we should be quite optimistic about the future. I have assured him that he will not need a colostomy.

Yours sincerely
Paul Newton
Consultant Geriatrician

24. FEMALE, AGED 25

Doctor: Well, Maureen, come and sit down. Your doctor says you've had pains in your tummy.[1] Tell me about them.

Patient: Yes, it started with that. It made me wonder if I was pregnant and then one day — it was a Saturday — I heard a voice telling me that I was going to have twins: one baby would be Satan[2] and the other Jesus.[3]

Doctor: Did you tell anyone about this?

Patient: Oh no, well, not for a long time. But I felt very low[4] and easily upset. If anything went wrong at the office, I flew off the handle.[5] My boss was really very nice about it.

Doctor: Do you get on well with your boss?

Patient: Yes — he's special to me.
He . . .

Doctor: How do you mean special?

Patient: Whenever he comes into the office I know he's been sent to look after me, protect me.

Doctor: Did he suggest you go to your GP?

Patient: No, I don't know why he didn't see I was scared[6] that if he got to know I was having a baby I should get the sack.[7] Whenever I went into the office I felt everyone staring at me and I felt they were all talking about me.

Doctor: Is there anyone in particular you don't like in the office?

Patient: Oh yes. Mrs Mulloney.

Doctor: Who is she?

Patient: She's the cleaner. I know she works for the Devil and she spies on me so I have to lock all my things away before I go home.

Doctor: Do you mean your work?

Patient: And my own belongings in case they get contaminated.

Doctor: So what made you finally go to your GP?

Patient: Well, my friend Pat thought I should go. She'd heard me talking to my voices.

Doctor: What do your voices say?

Patient: Sometimes they say, 'Maureen is the mother of God. She has been specially chosen . . . You must never look at another man . . .' I wanted to see a doctor and a priest too.

Doctor: Mm. Well now. Tell me about your family. Have you still got your parents?

Patient: I've got my Mum. She's sixty. She was a midwife and she now lives in Birmingham.

Doctor: And your father?

Patient: He died 7 months ago. He'd been ill for ages[8] with heart trouble.

Doctor: Did you get on well with your family?

Patient: I suppose so. They were rather cold though. It wasn't a cheerful, happy home like some people have.

Doctor: Have you any brothers or sisters?

Patient: No, I'm the only one.

Doctor: How did you get on at school?

Patient: Well, I was a bit lonely because we moved several times so I had to change schools a lot so never had any real friends. I felt a bit happier when I was at the Comprehensive School. I was good at sport.

Doctor: Did you make any friends through games?

Patient: Not really. I kept myself to myself. I never wanted to join in things even after matches like the others did.

Doctor: What did you do when you left school?

Patient: I did a short secretarial course at the College and then I got the job I have now.

Doctor: And how have you been managing with the job?

Patient: Just after I started, my father got a job in Birmingham but I decided to stay in London so moved into a bed-sitter[9] in Fulham . . . I often sit and cry for hours.

Doctor: When did your periods start?

Patient: When I was twelve.

Doctor: Have you had any steady boy friends?[10]

Patient: No. I'm not keen on that kind of thing.[11]

Doctor: Have you ever had any illnesses?

Patient: Only cold and flu and upset tummy. I feel rotten when I get my period.[12] I'm just starting one right now . . .

Doctor: I see. Well, I'd like to have a good look at you.

Physical examination

A healthy young woman who appeared to be slightly undernourished. Examination also confirmed that the patient was menstruating.

Mental state examination

Maureen was very restless and could not sit for more than a minute at a time. She was very distractable and on several occasions went to the window to look out at people in the street. Her hair was untidy. Her expression was one of bewilderment.

Speech

She said very little, and sometimes she had to be asked the same question twice. She was very preoccupied with her thoughts about her pregnancy and found it difficult to discuss anything else.

Cognitive testing

She was fully orientated for time, place and person. Her general knowledge was excellent as were her short and long-term recall.

Diagnosis

Acute schizophrenia.

Treatment

This young woman has never been ill before, lives alone and her abnormal beliefs and experiences are beginning to affect her behaviour towards others. She needs to be protected in a safe environment and, because she is not living with relatives, normally it would be necessary to admit her to a psychiatric ward in a hospital which has the necessary facilities for investigating the cause of her illness. This should include a wide range of physical, laboratory, social and psychological investigations. She will need nursing supervision, medication with major tranquillizers and she should also be encouraged to take care of herself as much as possible and be kept occupied through occupational therapy. Further treatment would depend on how well she responded to these measures.

Explanations

1. *tummy*: this word is used by patients to mean stomach or abdomen.
2. *Satan*: the Devil.
3. *Jesus*: Jesus Christ.
4. *low*: depressed.
5. *flew off the handle*: lost my temper.
6. *scared*: afraid.
7. *get the sack*: lose my job.
8. *for ages*: for a long time.
9. *a bed-sitter*: a room used for living and sleeping.
10. *steady boy friend*: a boy friend for a long period and may imply a sexual relationship.
11. *not keen on that kind of thing*: not interested in sex.
12. *period*: menstruation.

Letter to GP from Consultant

Institute of Psychiatry
De Crespigny Park
London SE5 BAF
2 3 95

Dr G Hornby
102 Fulham Road
SW6

Dear Doctor Hornby

Maureen Cleaver (F) 15 10 70, 35 Lillie Road SW6

Thank you very much for referring Maureen Cleaver to us. I agree with you that she does seem to be suffering from some of the initial symptoms of a schizophrenia-like illness. I have arranged for her to be admitted to one of our beds in the district general hospital. We will of course fully investigate her both physically and psychologically.

As you know she believes that she is pregnant with twins. She is not puzzled by the fact that she is also menstruating at present. She describes hearing voices which have said: 'Maureen is the mother of God. She has been specially chosen . . .' etc. She mentioned that she was unwell to a colleague at work who suggested that she see you.

Her mother is a 60-year-old retired widow living in Birmingham and her father died seven months ago. She was an only child and I gather that the family atmosphere was rather cold. I have been unable to establish whether there is any family history of mental illness. Her mother has not replied to my request to discuss Maureen's problems with her.

Maureen apparently had a normal birth and early development. She kept to herself at school and avoided sporting and other social occasions. She had an average level of academic performance and is currently in her first job as a secretary. Her menarche was at 12 years and she has had no sexual experiences. There is no previous medical or psychiatric history nor has there been any anti-social behaviour and she does not abuse drugs or alcohol.

She is physically well and nulliparous. She was very restless and could not sit still for more than a minute or two at a time. Her speech was logical though occasionally she became distracted. Her expression was blank and occasionally somewhat perplexed, but not frightened or depressed. She said that she had been feeling low-spirited and crying and she freely described the abnormal experiences and beliefs which I have mentioned, together with others of a more persecutory nature. She was fully orientated, had excellent short and long-term recall and had no difficulty with any of the copying and constructional tests that I asked her to do.

It is still too early to talk about long-term management and prognosis. Her illness is clearly functional, with an acute onset with some depressive features and one hopes that she will be rapidly restored and able to return to work. However, her general social isolation suggests a poor premorbid personality and even the possibility of a more insidious onset of a deteriorating process, which only time can make clear. I shall certainly keep you informed about her progress and, if an early discharge seems possible, I would like to discuss her with you.

Yours sincerely
Clifford Drummond
Consultant Psychiatrist

25. MAN, AGED 38

Referred by GP to Outpatients complaining of loss of weight, vomiting, oedema and nocturia.

Doctor: Good morning, Mr Hartley. Come and sit down. Well now, your doctor says you've been having trouble with your water[1] for some time.

Patient: Yes, that's right. I have to keep getting up[2] in the night.

Doctor: How many times?

Patient: Oh, up to six times lately.

Doctor: Have you noticed any change in your water?

Patient: Yes, it's darker, reddish. I wonder if it could be blood.

Doctor: Have you noticed anything else?

Patient: Yes. I've been sick[3] several times in the morning and after work in the evening I've noticed my legs are puffed up.[4]

Doctor: How is your general health?

Patient: Well, I've felt really groggy[5] for some weeks now. I don't seem to enjoy my food any more and I've lost weight.

Doctor: How much?

Patient: About a stone.[6] I can tell by my clothes and my wife's worried about it. She made me go to my doctor.

Doctor: How long have you had this trouble?

Patient: About 3 months really.

Doctor: Have you ever had trouble with your water before?

Patient: Yes. A couple of years ago I had burning when I passed water. The doctor said I had high blood pressure as well and he put me on tablets and it cleared up.[7]

Doctor: Well, I'd like to examine you. Take off all your clothes except your underpants. Lie on the couch under the blanket and I'll be with you in a moment.

After examining the patient:

Doctor: You can get dressed now . . . Well, Mr Hartley, I think your problem is due to the fact that the kidneys are not working as well as they should be. I want you to have some blood tests, X-rays and kidney function tests. I want you to collect your urine for 24 hours. Nurse will tell you exactly how to do it. Then we'll ask you to come in for an ultrasound examination of the kidneys. This is a very simple procedure to make sure there is no obstruction.

Follow-up clinic.

Doctor: Hello, Mr Hartley. Come and sit down. Well, as I told you, the kidneys are not working as well as they should be. I'm going to send you to a dietitian and she will give you advice on a low protein diet. This is not unpleasant[8] and it will lower the chemicals in your blood. It is the protein in the diet that causes a build-up of substances in the blood when the kidneys are not working normally. This makes you feel unwell. I'm also going to give you some tablets to help to keep the bones healthy. This is necessary in people with kidney disease.

Patient: Can you tell me exactly what is wrong with my kidneys?

Doctor: Well, the tests show that it is probably a condition called chronic glomerulonephritis which has damaged the kidneys. The condition is irreversible[9] — nothing can be done to put it right at this stage I'm afraid.[10] You've undoubtedly had it for a long time. We'll need to keep an eye on you.[11] There are fortunately treatments to make up for the kidney damage.

Some weeks later.

Doctor: I gather[12] you've been having more trouble since I last saw you?

Patient: Oh yes. I've kept vomiting and feeling dreadful.[13] I can't keep on like this.[14]

Doctor: Mmm. Well, it looks as though the next step will be to get you into hospital to start further treatment. I think you are going to need peritoneal dialysis treatment.

Patient: What's that Doctor?

Doctor: It means putting a tube into the abdomen and then washing fluid in and out to keep the toxic substances in the blood down. It's not uncomfortable and you'll be taught to do it yourself for when you get home.

Patient:	How long will I have to stay in hospital?
Doctor:	You'll be in from 2–3 weeks. With this method of dialysis you can walk about and live a reasonably normal life.
Patient:	Shall I have to stop working, Doctor?
Doctor:	Just remind me. What do you do?[15]
Patient:	I'm a bus conductor.
Doctor:	Well I think it might prove difficult for you. I'd advise you to get a lighter job but we'll see how you get on.[16]
Patient:	Shall I have to use this for the rest of my life?
Doctor:	Well, there are changes and improvements in treatment all the time. We will take a specimen of your blood and put you on the computer for a kidney transplant. When a suitable kidney comes, we will do a kidney transplant operation. This will make life a lot easier and there are new drugs now to prevent the body rejecting the new kidney. So there are several ways of helping you. We'll just have to see how you get on.
Patient:	Thank you Doctor.

Explanations

1. *water*: urine.
2. *keep getting up*: frequently get out of bed to urinate.
3. *been sick*: vomited.
4. *puffed up*: swollen.
5. *groggy*: unwell.
6. *a stone*: roughly 6.34 kilos (see page xv).
7. *cleared up*: got better.
8. *not unpleasant*: in English when you have two negatives, known as a double negative, it creates a middle way, meaning not a positive, 'a pleasant diet', but not a negative, 'an unpleasant diet'. So here, '*not un*pleasant' means a fairly acceptable diet.
9. *irreversible*: it is best to avoid phrases like this when speaking to most patients. Here the doctor quickly explains in more simple language what an irreversible condition means.

10. *I'm afraid*: these words signal to the patient regret. The phrase 'I'm afraid' is used to introduce news which is unwelcome, bad.
11. *keep an eye on you*: keep a frequent check on you.
12. *gather*: understand, believe.
13. *feeling dreadful*: an emotional phrase to express feeling very unwell.
14. *can't keep on like this*: can't continue in this condition.
15. *what do you do?*: what is your job?
16. *you get on*: you progress.

26. MAN, AGED 36

Follow-up in Cardiac Clinic. Junior doctor present with Consultant.

Doctor: Hello again, Mr Waites. We met last week, didn't we? I've been telling my colleague here about you. I've seen the results of the tests but there are just one or two points I'd like you to clarify for me and for the benefit of Dr Granger. You did say that this pain and discomfort has troubled you for nearly 8 months and is getting worse?

Patient: That's right, Doctor. And since I saw you last week I had a really bad turn[1] after breakfast.

Doctor: Can I get you to describe the character of the pain — or in other words, tell us what it is like exactly?

Patient: It is not always a pain as such; often just a feeling of discomfort in the chest, like someone pressing on my chest.

Doctor: Does the discomfort go anywhere else?

Patient: Not really, although I do get a numbness in my leg with it.

Doctor: Last week you mentioned that it often came on when walking but not always. Can you remember what you are most commonly doing when it comes on?

Patient: I've been thinking about that since you asked me the last time I was here and usually it's after my evening meal and when I go to bed at night. I've also noticed it when I have sex with my wife. I very rarely get it at work.

Doctor: Well, it seems to me that perhaps the pain comes on as often when you are not exercising as when you are.

Patient: Yes, I'm sure that's true, Doctor.

Doctor: Could you just remind me what else you notice when you get this pain?

Patient: Like I told you last time, I do get palpitations[2] sometimes.

Doctor: By which you mean?

Patient: A strong banging in my chest as if my heart was going to come out.

Doctor: What about your breathing when you have the pain?

Patient:	I don't notice any difference.
Doctor:	Now what would happen if you and I went for a walk up the hill to the station?
Patient:	What now?
Doctor:	No, I just meant if we were to walk what do you think would happen? Could you keep up with[3] me if I walked fast?
Patient:	Oh yes. Last summer I climbed Ben Nevis.[4]
Doctor:	Mmm. Well, as I said, we've had the result of the tests and this discussion today has been very helpful. I'm happy to be able to reassure you about your heart which is essentially normal apart from one minor problem. One of the valves of your heart (and you've got four) leaks a little. This leaking produces an extra noise in the heart which we call a heart murmur. Although there is this murmur there, it doesn't interfere with the functioning of your heart and I'm quite sure it won't interfere with your enjoyment of life or length of life.
Patient:	Is there anything you can do about it?
Doctor:	Well, although we could give you medication for the palpitations, it isn't really necessary as they are not in the least bit dangerous. They're a nuisance but they may disappear of their own accord. So what I'm really saying is; this is a nuisance but only a nuisance. It's not dangerous and I want you to lead an entirely normal life. Do anything you want to do. The only one precaution is to tell any surgeon who wants to do an operation or dentist who wants to take out a tooth that you do need an antibiotic in order to prevent any infection getting on to the leaking valve. Well now, Mr Waites. Is there anything you'd like to ask me?[5]
Patient:	Do you think I've had this since birth?
Doctor:	No, I don't think so but it is possible you were born with a tendency to develop this problem. Right, Mr Waites, I'll write to your doctor about all this. I don't think I need to see you on a regular basis as there's nothing

seriously wrong but I'd be happy to see you again if your
doctor would like you to.

Patient: Thank you Doctor. That's a relief.

Explanations:

1. *a bad turn*: an attack of symptoms.
2. *palpitations*: this word is used by patients to mean different things
   so the doctor asks for clarification.
3. *keep up with*: walk as fast as.
4. *Ben Nevis*: the highest mountain in the UK.
5. This is a good question to ask patients to give them an opportunity
   of expressing fears, seeking clearer explanations, etc.

Letter to GP from Consultant

Cardiology Department
Royal Victoria Infirmary
Newcastle upon Tyne
7 December 1992

Dr Crisp
Abbotts Health Centre
14 Crispin Way
Newcastle upon Tyne

Dear Dr Crisp

R Waites (M) 4 6 56, 15 Faber Road Newcastle upon Tyne

Thank you for asking me to see this man and for your helpful letter
about him. He gives a history of chest discomfort which has been
present for 8 months and is getting progressively worse. Although
the chest discomfort usually occurs with exercise it can occur after
eating and after sexual intercourse. The pain is sometimes associated
with palpitation but he has not noticed any associated shortness of
breath.

In the past he had pneumonia as a child and has also had an
appendicectomy. I note that he smokes quite heavily and drinks a
bottle of whisky per week. There is no family history of coronary
artery disease.

On examination he is normotensive and there is no evidence of heart
failure. His pulse is 80 regular and of normal character. His apex
beat is normal on auscultation. He has normal heart sounds but has
a late systolic murmur, maximal at the apex. It radiates to the left
sternal edge. The remainder of the physical examination is normal
and there are no stigmata of infective endocarditis or of liver disease.
His investigations show a normal chest X-ray. His resting ECG
shows some non-specific ST segment and T-wave changes in the
inferior leads. It is otherwise normal. His echocardiogram shows a

normal left ventricular cavity, normal aorta and left atrium. The pattern movement of the mitral valve suggests a prolapse of the valve. The left ventricular wall movements are quite normal.

I think it is likely that this man has a myxomatous degeneration of his mitral valve which is causing mitral regurgitation. This is of no haemodynamic importance and he should be encouraged to lead an entirely normal life. The only precaution he needs is for antibiotic cover for any potentially septic procedures.

Yours sincerely
Dr P Stevens MD FRCP
Consultant Physician & Cardiologist

27. MAN, AGED 45

Doctor:	Good morning Mr Carter. I'm Dr Hartley. Dr Walters has asked me to see you and has sent me a letter. Shall we go through things together? How old are you?
Patient:	Forty five.
Doctor:	Tell me how long you've been unwell.
Patient:	Well, I've had a sore mouth for six months and I started losing weight four months ago.
Doctor:	Any other problems?
Patient:	Well, I've been sweating, especially at night.
Doctor:	How bad is the sweating?
Patient:	Bad enough to wet the sheets.
Doctor:	Have you had a cough?
Patient:	No.
Doctor:	Have you ever had TB or been in contact with anyone with TB?
Patient:	One of my friends died of AIDS and he had TB.
Doctor:	I see. Would you consider yourself at risk from HIV?
Patient:	Well, I've been very careful over the last three years but before that I used to be quite promiscuous.[1]
Doctor:	Have you ever had any sexually transmitted diseases, like gonorrhoea?
Patient:	Yes, I had gonorrhoea ten years ago. I was treated for it at St Mary's Hospital.
Doctor:	Have you ever had herpes?
Patient:	No.
Doctor:	Were you having sex with your friend who died of AIDS?
Patient:	No, but we did have a joint lover.
Doctor:	Have you been worrying about being infected with HIV?
Patient:	Yes, when I started to lose weight and got the night sweats. I knew they were the same symptoms my friend got.
Doctor:	Have you discussed this properly with anyone else?
Patient:	I talked a bit about it with Dr Walters but he said it was best to see you.

Doctor:	Have you been in contact with the Terence Higgins Trust[2] or any other voluntary bodies?
Patient:	No.
Doctor:	Is there anything else you'd like to tell me at this stage?
Patient:	No. I've no other problems.
Doctor:	Can you tell me if you are taking any medicine of any kind?
Patient:	I've been taking live yoghurt because I thought I had thrush[3] in my mouth.
Doctor:	Do you smoke or drink?
Patient:	I don't smoke and I only have alcohol occasionally.
Doctor:	Well, I'd like to examine you.

Clinical examination

Doctor:	You have sore patches on the corner of your mouth. How long have you had them?
Patient:	For six months.
Doctor:	So you still have thrush in your mouth. Has the yoghurt helped?
Patient:	I think so.
Doctor:	Have you noticed any skin rashes?
Patient:	Yes, my face has gone dry. There's also a patch under my arm.
Doctor:	This rash around your anus looks like herpes. How long have you had it?
Patient:	A month.
Doctor:	You can get dressed now.

After patient is dressed:

Doctor:	Your GP wonders whether you want to be tested for HIV. How do you feel about it?
Patient:	I'm very frightened. Do you think some of my problems could be related to AIDS?
Doctor:	Yes, I'm afraid that some of the skin changes and the candida and the soreness at the side of your mouth are commonly seen in people who are HIV positive.

Patient: Yes, I was afraid you'd say that. Well, we might as well get on with the test then.

Doctor: Well, I want to discuss some other issues first. Do you understand the difference between AIDS and HIV positive?

Patient: Not really.

Doctor: The antibody only tells us that you have at some time been infected by the virus. It does not tell us anything about what is happening to you now or what will happen in the future. It is very important to know how you would handle this information if it comes back positive. Who would support you?

Patient: I don't know. My parents don't even know I'm gay.[4] I wouldn't want them to know. My brother knows I'm not very well. He might be willing to help me.

Doctor: Would you like to speak to a colleague of mine who is very helpful as a counsellor?

Patient: Yes.

Doctor: I could also give you the phone number of the Terence Higgins Trust and other organisations.

Patient: I'm not really interested as I'm not into the gay scene, strange as it may seem.

Doctor: If I do the blood test today I shall not have the results for up to two weeks. Do you think you'll be able to cope with the delay?

Patient: Yes. How will you send it to me?

Doctor: I'll want you to come back. We never give this information except person-to-person even if it is negative. I'd like to talk to you about things like mortgages and life insurance. Do you understand that if I take this blood test it could jeopardise your chances of a life insurance and getting a mortgage?

Patient: Well, I didn't know that but it doesn't worry me. I'd like to have the blood test.

Clinical notes

O/E   eczematous rash round nose and mouth/angular cheilosis.
          Red area 10 cm in l. axilla.
          No other rash except dandruff in scalp.

BP $\dfrac{130}{80}$

P   90
Chest   clear
Abdomen   NAD
Soft nodes up to 1 cm diameter both sides of neck and both groins.
Peri-anal skin: reddened, inflamed. ? herpetic.

Return visit two weeks later

Doctor: Good morning Mr Carter. Come and sit down.

Patient: I've brought my brother with me.

Doctor: Good. How've you been?

Patient: Worse, much worse. I started feeling as if I had flu the day after I saw you and it's no better.

Doctor: Tell me about it. Have you a cough?

Patient: Yes.

Doctor: Do you bring up any sputum?

Patient: No.

Doctor: Have you had any fevers?

Patient: Yes and bad sweats. I had one coming in the car just now and I was absolutely drenched.

Doctor: Do you get out of breath?

Patient: Oh yes. I can't walk upstairs as easily as I could. I notice if I take a deep breath it makes me cough.

Doctor: Could you do that now? (Patient takes deep breath and coughs.)

Doctor: Has anything else changed?

Patient: No, my weight's steady.

Doctor: Any diarrhoea?

Patient: No.

Doctor: I want to listen to your chest. (Auscultates chest.) Good. That's clear. I'd like to see how far you can walk upstairs.

Let's go into the passage. (Patient walks up 15 steps and is then gasping for breath. Returns to room.)

Doctor: So, you are much less fit than you were two months ago?

Patient: Yes, three or four weeks ago I could have climbed much further.

Doctor: Right. I would like you to go for an X-ray now. Are you worried that this is PCP?

Patient: What's PCP?

Doctor: I'm sorry. It is pneumocystis pneumonia.

Patient: Isn't that AIDS? Was my blood test positive?

Doctor: I'm afraid it was and if you do have PCP that would mean you have AIDS.

Brother: Is there any treatment for it?

Doctor: Yes, we would admit your brother and start him on treatment with an antibiotic called co-trimoxazole. If he can take this by mouth, he can take some of it in the Outpatient Clinic but it does make some patients feel very sick.

X-ray showed reticular nodular shadowing consistent with PCP. Patient admitted. Started on treatment which proved beneficial.

Explanations

1. *to be promiscuous*: to have casual sexual relations with many people.
2. *Terence Higgins Trust*: this is a major charitable organisation offering advice and help to HIV positive people. There are other organisations such as Body Positive and Frontliners.
3. *thrush*: candida.
4. *gay*: homosexual.

28. WOMAN, AGED 60

Diabetic, previously had bleeding ulcer treated with Zantac. Referred by GP complaining of pain all over body.

Doctor: Your GP says you're getting pain all over your body.

Patient: Yes. I was brought here by ambulance in 1968. I was in agony[1] for weeks and months. I've had a collar and a surgical corset but I'm still in pain.

Doctor: How often do you get the pain?

Patient: Every moment of the day I have pain from top to toe.

Doctor: If you had to point to one place where it is worst, where would it be?

Patient: My back. In 1972 they removed a cyst from my toe. They gave me an injection in my spine. The following day I had bleeding from down below.[2] I was in hospital one month. Since that time I've had pain in my back. I take paracetamol. They told me it was spondylitis in my neck. They gave me heat treatment and a collar. I used it for years.

Doctor: Do you have any tingling of the feet or hands?

Patient: Yes, I'm diabetic. I feel pins and needles.

Doctor: How are the waterworks?[3]

Patient: All right.

Doctor: Bowels?

Patient: All right.

Doctor: Have you had any operations?

Patient: No. Only appendix.

Doctor: When did you last have your back X-rayed?

Patient: Long ago.

Doctor: Are you taking any tablets?

Patient: I take 26 units of insulin for my diabetes. I have Zantac for my ulcer, tablets for my hay fever and also two glibenclamide for my diabetes.

Doctor: Who looks after your diabetes?

Patient: Dr Holman at St Mary's. I've put on so much weight.[4] They want me to go on a diet.

Doctor: Come through this way. Take off everything to your

underwear. (Patient undresses.) I'm going to start off
by examining your hands.

Patient: They're very painful.

Doctor: Are they worse in the morning or evening?

Patient: Morning. I do a bit of housework and I get pain.

Doctor: Are you stiff? Put your hands above your head. Good.
Now behind your back. Swing your legs onto the couch.
Where does it hurt? Just relax. Bend the legs. Can you
feel me touching them? Do both sides feel the same?
Now lie on your tummy and I'll look at your back. Roll
over. I'm just going to pummel[5] your back a bit. Tell me
if it hurts.

Patient: When I lie down like this the pain is so bad I grip my
hands. I don't know what to do.

After the clinical examination, the patient dressed.

Doctor: Well, I'm going to get some blood tests done to see what
is causing the pain in your joints. I'll also get an X-ray
of your back.

Patient: They said it was osteo-arthritis.

Doctor: Yes, well there is very little we can do for that. I'm going
to refer you to the Pain Relief Clinic. It is run by[6] an
anaesthetist. He has a lot of experience with pain and
may be able to offer you advice. I'll write to your doctor
and tell him I've seen you.

Explanations

1. *in agony*: in extreme pain.
2. *bleeding from down below*: vaginal bleeding.
3. *waterworks*: bladder.
4. *put on weight*: weight has increased.
5. *to pummel*: strike (usually with the fist).
6. *run by*: managed by.

29. WOMAN, AGED 69

Patient complaining of severe pain in right arm and right leg. Follow-up clinic.

Doctor: How've you been, Mrs Cooper?

Patient: Terrible, terrible.

Doctor: I'm sorry. Let me see. How long is it since I saw you?

Patient: It's three months. I had two lots of physiotherapy but it gave me terrible pain.

Doctor: Did we do an X-ray?

Patient: Yes, of my neck.

Doctor: Yes, here it is. You've got a bit of arthritis. How did you get on with the tablets?[1]

Patient: Oh, I can't take them. They made me feel sick.[2] The only ones I can take are paracetamol.

Doctor: Well, take off your clothes so I can see your shoulder and neck.

O/E

Doctor: Is the pain on all the time or only when you walk?

Patient: Nearly all the time.

Doctor: Put your arms above your head. Does that hurt?

Patient: No.

Doctor: Is that tender?

Patient: No.

Doctor: Is the pain in the joints worse in the mornings?

Patient: Yes.

Doctor: Any tingling in the hands and feet?

Patient: A little in the feet.

Doctor: What about the waterworks?[3]

Patient: I go more than I used to.[4]

Doctor: Do you have full control?

Patient: Yes.

Doctor: Bowels?

Patient: All right.

Doctor: Do your feet feel they're not really on the ground?

Patient: Sometimes.

Doctor:	Let me look at your feet. Just relax. Can you feel me touching you? Does that feel hot or cold?
Patient:	Cold.
Doctor:	Do your feet feel cold all the time?
Patient:	Yes.
Doctor:	Hold the leg up and push down. Press down as hard as you can. Now relax the leg. Let your legs go loose and relax. Let your foot drop. I'm going to scratch the bottom of your feet. Does it feel the same both sides? Does that feel hot or cold?
Patient:	Yes. They feel cold.
Doctor:	What do you feel there?
Patient:	Tingling.
Doctor:	Sit up. I'll look at your neck. The pain is there, is it?
Patient:	Yes.
Doctor:	If I touch you here, does that feel normal?
Patient:	Yes.
Doctor:	Well, there's nothing wrong with the nerves. All the nerves are working perfectly well. But maybe one of the nerves is irritated. Which joints give you most trouble?
Patient:	My arm.
Doctor:	Well, what I could do would be to give you an injection. It often helps to relieve joint pain. How do you feel about that?
Patient:	Could it help the pain?
Doctor:	Yes. Shall I try? It's up to you.[5] It won't do any harm. It's just like a blood test.
Patient:	Yes, I'll have it.

Doctor gives patient an injection of steroid into the shoulder joint.

Doctor:	I'll put a plaster on. That will be a bit sore. Take a paracetamol. You should feel better tomorrow. You can get dressed now. I'll see you in six weeks.

Explanations

1. *How did you get on with the tablets?*: Were the drugs beneficial?
2. *feel sick*: have nausea.
3. *waterworks*: bladder.
4. *I go more than I used to*: I pass more water nowadays.
5. *It's up to you*: you must decide.

6 Medical abbreviations

The rapid development of medicine and the related sciences in recent years has brought a vast increase in medical vocabulary. At the same time, the increased speed of life has driven people to use abbreviations more and more and this tendency is well illustrated in the medical and scientific field.

Abbreviations are disliked and discouraged by many doctors because they are variable and misleading. The choice between capital and small letters and the use of the full stop (e.g. A.C. rather than AC) is often a personal one. The same initials may have different meanings in different medical fields.

Nevertheless, abbreviations *are* used every day in medical reports, on record cards and case histories and in speech, and a knowledge of them is, therefore, absolutely essential.

A SELECTION OF ABBREVIATIONS COMMONLY USED BY THE MEDICAL PROFESSION IN THE UK

A

A acute; anterior; artery; attendance.

A₃, A₇ to attend surgery in three, seven days.

aa (Greek: of each) used to show the same quantity of each ingredient in a prescription.

AAS anthrax antiserum.

ABG arterial blood gas.

AC air conduction; alternating current; anodal closure.

a.c. ante cibum (Latin) before meals.

ACE angiotensin converting enzyme.

ACTH adrenocorticotrophic hormone.

ADL activities of daily life.

A/E. Accident and Emergency Department.

Aet aetas (Latin) age.

AF atrial fibrillation.

A/Gratio albumin/globulin ratio.

AHA Area Health Authority.

AI aortic incompetence; aortic insufficiency; artificial insemination.

AID artificial insemination by donor.

AIDS acquired immune deficiency syndrome.

Alb albumin.

ALP alkaline phosphatase.

ALT alanine transaminase.

Amb ambulance.

AMOH Association of Medical Officers of Health.

amp ampere; amputation.

AN antenatal.

ANF antinuclear factor.

ANS autonomic nervous system.

AP antero-posterior; artificial pneumothorax.

APH antepartum haemorrhage.

APN artificial pneumothorax.

ARC AIDS-related complex.

ARF acute renal failure.

ARM artificial rupture of membranes.

AS alimentary system; anxiety state; aortic stenosis.

ASD atrial septal defect.

ASO antistreptolysin O.

AST aspartate transaminase.

ATN acute tubular necrosis.

AVC atrio-ventricular-canal.

A & W alive and well.

AXR abdominal X-ray.

AZT azidothymidine (Zidovudine).

Å angstrom unit.

B

B brother.

Ba E barium enema.

Ba M barium meal.

BB bed bath; blanket bath.

BBA born before arrival.

BBD baby born dead.

BCG bacille Calmette Guérin.

b.d. twice a day.

BF breast fed.

BI bone injury.

BID brought in dead.

b.i.d. bis in die (Latin) Twice a day.

BIH bilateral inguinal hernias.

BM bowel movement.

BMA British Medical Association.

BMR basal metabolic rate.

BNA Basle Nomina Anatomica.

BNF British National Formulary.

BNO bowels not opened.

BO body odour; bowels opened.

BOR bowels opened regularly.

BP blood pressure; British Pharmacopoeia.

BPC British Pharmaceutical Codex.

Br bronchitis; brown.

BRCS British Red Cross Society.

BS breath sounds; blood sugar.

B'sp bronchospasm.

B Wt birth weight.

C

C carbon; cathode; centigrade; (temperature scale); certificate; cervical; consultation.

C 1 – 8 cervical spine segments.

CAPD continuous ambulatory peritoneal dialysis.

CBD common bile duct.

Cf first certificate.

C$_1$, C$_4$, C$_{13}$ intermediate certificate for 1, 4, 13 weeks.

CF final certificate.

Cp private certificate.

c. circa (Latin) about.

c. with.

Ca carcinoma.

CAL chronic airways limitation.

CAO chronic airways obstruction.

CC chest clinic; creatinine clearance.

cc cubic centimetre.

CCF congestive cardiac failure.

CD Controlled Drugs

CDH congenital dislocation of hips.

cen centimetres.

CF cardiac failure.

CFA cryptogenic fibrosing alveolitis.

CFT complement fixation test.

Cgh cough.

Ch child; children; chronic.

CHD congenital heart disease.

Cho/Vac cholera vaccine.

CI colour index

Circ circulation; circumcision.

cm centimetre.

CMV cytomegalovirus.

CNS central nervous system.

CO Casualty Officer.

C/O complains of.

COAD chronic obstructive airways disease.

C of H circumference of head.

Comp complemented.

Conj conjunctivitis.

COP change of plaster.

CP colour perception.

C'p chickenpox.

CPK creatinine phosphokinase.

CPR cardiopulmonary resuscitation.

CRF chronic renal failure.

CSA child sexual abuse.

CSF cerebrospinal fluid.

CSSD Central Sterile Supply Depot.

CSU catheter specimen of urine.

CT computed tomography

CV cardiovascular; cervical vertebra; colour vision; conversational voice; curriculum vitae.

CVA cerebrovascular accident.

CVP central venous pressure.

CVS cardiovascular system.

Cx cervix.

C.XR chest X-ray.

Cyl cylinder.

Cz coryza.

D

d density; dioptre; dorsal; dose.

D/- daily total in divided doses.

D 1 – 12 dorsal spine segments.

DA dental anaesthetic.

DAO Duly Authorised Officer.

D & C dilatation and curettage.

DCR dacro-cysto-rhinostomy.

D & D drunk & disorderly.

DED date expected delivery.

Derm dermatitis.

DH drug history; Department of Health.

DIC died in Casualty; disseminated intravascular coagulation.

Dip diphtheria.

Dip/Vac/FT diphtheria prophylactic formol toxoid.

DLE disseminated lupus erythematosus.

DMO Divisional Medical Officer.

DMR Duty Medical Registrar.

DN district nurse.

DNA deoxyribonucleic acid; did not attend.

DNKA did not keep appointment.

DNS deflected nasal septum; did not suit.

DOA dead on arrival.

DOB date of birth.

DOM Dept. of Medicine.

DOS Dept. of Surgery.

DP/Vac diphtheria pertussis prophylactic vaccine.

DPP diphtheria pertussis prophylactic.

DS disseminated sclerosis; double strength.

D Sph dioptre spherical.

DSR Duty Surgical Registrar.

DT delirium tremens; diphtheria and tetanus; distance test.

DT/Vac diphtheria tetanus vaccine.

DTN diphtheria toxin normal.

DTP diphtheria, tetanus and pertussis.

DU duodenal ulcer.
Dup duplicate.
DV domiciliary visit.
DVT deep venous thrombosis.
D & V diarrhoea and vomiting.
DXR deep X-ray radiation.
DXT deep X-ray therapy.
Dysm dysmenorrhoea.
△ diagnosis
† died.

E

E evening.
EAA extrinsic allergic alveolitis.
EBS emergency bed service.
ECF extracellular fluid.
ECG electrocardiogram.
ECT electroconvulsive therapy.
EDC expected date of confinement.
EDD expected date of delivery.
EDM early diastolic murmur.
EEG electroencephalogram.
EENT eyes, ears, nose and throat.
EMU early morning specimen of urine.
ETT examination in theatre.
ENT ears, nose and throat.
EOM external ocular movement.
ERCP endoscopic retrograde cholangio-pancreatography.
ERPC evacuation of retained products of conception.

ES enema saponis.
ESM ejection systolic murmur.
ESN educationally sub-normal.
ESR erythrocyte sedimentation rate.
ESRD endstage renal disease.
ETT exercise tolerance test.
EUA examination under anaesthesia.
Ez eczema.

F

F Fahrenheit (temperature scale); father; female.
FA fatty acid; fibrosing alveolitis.
FB foreign body.
FBC full blood count.
FBS fasting blood sugar.
FH family history; fetal heart.
FHH fetal heart heard.
FHNH fetal heart not heard.
Fib fibrositis; fibula
f.m. fiat mistura (Latin) — make a mixture
FMF fetal movement felt.
FMP first menstrual period.
FP food poisoning.
FPC family planning clinic; family practitioner committee.
FT formol toxoid; full term.
FTA fluorescent treponemal antibody.
FTBD fit to be detained; full term born dead.

FTND full term normal delivery.
FW forced whisper.

G

γ **GT** gamma glutaryl transferase.
g gram(s); gramme(s).
GA general anaesthetic; general attention.
G and A gas and air.
GB gallbladder.
GBM glomerular basement membrane.
GC general condition; gonococcus.
GCFT gonococcal complement fixation test.
GFR glomerular filtration rate.
GI gastrointestinal.
GIFT gamete intra-fallopian transfer.
GIT gastrointestinal tract.
GMC General Medical Council.
GP general practitioner.
GPC general physical condition.
GPI general paralysis of the insane.
GTT glucose tolerance test.
GU gastric ulcer; genitourinary.
Gyn gynaecology.

H

H hospital, hydrogen.

Hb haemoglobin.
HBD hydroxy-butarate dehydrogenase.
HC head circumference; hydrocortisone.
HF Hageman factor.
HI head injury.
HIV human immunodeficiency virus.
HLA human leucocytes antigen.
H of F height of fundus.
HM head movements.
HNPU has not passed urine.
HP House Physician.
HPC history of presenting complaint.
HRO Hospital Resettlement Officer.
hrs hours.
HS heart sounds; House Surgeon.
Ht heart; height.
H/T hypertension.

I

IBS irritable bowel syndrome.
ICF intracellular fluid.
ID infectious disease.
IM intramuscular.
Impr improved.
IOFB intra-ocular foreign body.
IP inpatient; insurance patient; interphalangeal.
IQ intelligence quotient.
IRL infra-red light.

IRU industrial rehabilitation unit.
ISQ in status quo.
IU international unit.
IUD intra-uterine device.
IV intravenous.
IVF in vitro fertilisation.
IVP intravenous pyelogram.
IVU intravenous urogram.
IVUD intravenous uro-dynamogram.
IZS insulin zinc suspension.

J

JVP jugular venous pressure.

K

KUB kidney, ureter and bladder.

L

l litre
Ⓛ left
L 1 – 5 lumbar spine segments.
Lab laboratory.
LA left atrium; local anaesthetic; local authority.
LAD left anterior descending (of coronary artery); left axis deviation.
LAH left anterior hemiblock.
lb pound (of weight).
LBBB left bundle branch block.

LBP low back pain.
LCA left coronary artery.
LDA left dorso-anterior position of the fetus.
LDH lactic dehydrogenase.
LDP left dorso-posterior position of the fetus.
LE left eye.
LE cells lupus erythematosus cells.
LFA left fronto-anterior position of fetus.
LFP left fronto-posterior position of the fetus.
LHA Local Health Authority.
LIF left iliac fossa.
LIH left inguinal hernia.
LLL left lower lobe
LLZ left lower zone.
LMA left mento-anterior position of fetus.
LMC local medical committee.
LMN lower motor neurone.
LMP last menstrual period; left mento-posterior position of fetus.
LMZ left middle zone.
LOA left occipito-anterior position of fetus.
LOP left occipito-posterior position of fetus.
LP lumbar puncture.
LPH left posterior hemiblock.
LSCS lower segment Caesarean section.
LSE left sternal edge.
LUA left upper arm.
LUZ left upper zone.

LV left ventricle; lumbar vertebra.

LVA left visual acuity.

LVF left ventricular failure.

LVH left ventricular hypertrophy.

M

M male; malignant; morning; mother.

mane in the morning (of drugs).

M and CW maternity and child welfare.

M/F; M/W/S male/female; married/widow(er)/single.

Mc millicurie(s).

MCH mean corpuscular haemoglobin.

MCHC mean corpuscular haemoglobin concentration.

MCL mid-clavicular line.

MCV mean corpuscular volume.

MDM mid-diastolic murmur.

mEq milliequivalent(s).

MHO Medical Health Officer.

MI mitral incompetence or insufficiency; myocardial infarction.

Misc miscarriage; miscellaneous.

MMR mass miniature radiography.

MO Medical Officer.

MOH Medical Officer of Health.

MOM milk of magnesia.

MOP medical outpatient.

MR manual removal; mitral regurgitation.

MRC Medical Research Council.

MRI magnetic resonance imaging.

MRU Mass radiography unit.

MS mitral stenosis; multiple sclerosis; musculo skeletal.

MSU mid stream urine.

MSW Medical Social Worker.

mμ millimicron(s).

MWO Mental Welfare Officer.

M.XR mass X-ray.

μ micron.

μg microgram(s).

N

N̄ or Ⓝ normal.

NA National Assistance; not applicable.

NAD no abnormality detected.

NAH not at home.

NAI non-accidental injury.

NBI no bone injury.

ND normal delivery; not diagnosed; not done.

NE not enlarged.

NFA no fixed abode; no further action.

NFV no further visit.

NG new growth; no good.

NGU non-gonococcal urethritis.

NI National Insurance.

NIC National Insurance Certificate; National Insurance Contributions.

NIL not in labour

nocte in the evening (of drugs).

NK not known.

NM neuromuscular.

NMR nuclear magnetic resonance.

NND neo-natal death.

NOTB National Ophthalmic Treatment Board.

NP nomen proprium.

NPU not passed urine.

NS nervous system; not seen.

NSAID non-steroidal anti-inflammatory drug.

NSPCC National Society for the Prevention of Cruelty to Children.

NSU non-specific urethritis.

N & T nose and throat.

N & V nausea and vomiting.

NYD not yet diagnosed.

NYK not yet known.

O

OA osteo-arthritis.

OAP old age pensioner.

Occ occasionally.

ODQ on direct questioning to systems review.

O/E, OE on examination; otitis externa.

OM omne mane (every morning); osteomyelitis; otitis media.

ON omne nocte (every evening).

Op operation.

OPA outpatient appointment.

OPD outpatients department.

OT occupational therapy; old tuberculin.

P

P pulse.

PA pernicious anaemia; posteroanterior; pressure area.

Paed paediatric.

PAN polyarteritis nodosa.

Para 0 + 0 (2 + 1) Formula meaning: P (number of pregnancies); a (number of abortions); ra (number of living children); no live pregnancy + no non-viable pregnancy; (two live children + one non-viable).

PAT paroxysmal atrial tachycardia.

PBI protein bound iodine.

PBZ phenylbutazone.

PCN percutaneous nephrostomy.

PCNL percutaneous nephrostomy lithotomy.

PD peritoneal dialysis.

PDA patent ductus arteriosus.

PE pulmonary embolus.

PEEP positive end expiratory pressure.

Pen penicillin.

PET pre-eclamptic toxaemia.

PFR peak flow rate.

PGL persistent generalised lymphadenopathy.

PH public health.

pH symbol for expression of hydrogen ion concentration.

Phy pharyngitis; physician.

PHLS Public Health Laboratory Service.

PI pulmonary insufficiency.

PID pelvic inflammatory disease; prolapsed intervertebral disc.

PL perception of light.

PM post-mortem.

PMB postmenopausal bleeding.

PMH past medical history.

PMP previous menstrual period.

PN postnatal.

PND paroxysmal nocturnal dyspnoea.

p.o. per os (Latin) by mouth.

PO, P Op, Post-op post-operative; post-operation.

POP Plaster of Paris.

PP private patient.

PPD progressive perceptive deafness.

PPH postpartum haemorrhage.

PR per rectum.

p.r.n. pro re nata (L) as required.

Prem premature

PS per speculum; pulmonary stenosis.

PSM pansystolic murmur.

Pt patient.

PT physical training; pulmonary tuberculosis.

PTA prior to admission.

PTB pulmonary tuberculosis.

PU passed urine; peptic ulcer.

PUO pyrexia of unknown or uncertain origin.

PUVA photochemical ultra violet light — A waves.

PV per vaginam.

PVT paroxysmal ventricular tachycardia.

PZI protamine zinc insulin.

Q

q.i.d. quater in die (Latin) four times a day.

q.d.s. four times a day.

R

r röntgen.

R red; respiration.

℞ recipe (Latin) take (used in prescriptions).

Ⓡ right.

RA rheumatoid arthritis; right atrium.

RAD right axis deviation.

RBC red blood cell count; red blood corpuscles.

RBS random blood sugar.
RE right eye.
Rh Rhesus factor; rheumatism.
RHA Regional Health Authority.
RIF right iliac fossa.
RIH right inguinal hernia.
RLL right lower lobe.
RLZ right lower zone.
RML right middle lobe.
RMO Regional or Resident Medical Officer.
RMZ right middle zone.
RNA ribonucleic acid.
ROA right occipital anterior.
ROO Resident Obstetric Officer.
ROP right occipital posterior.
ROS removal of sutures.
Rpt repeat; report.
RR respiratory rate.
RS respiratory system.
RSO Resident Surgical Officer.
RTA road traffic accident.
RTI respiratory tract infection.
RUA right upper arm.
RUL right upper lobe.
RUZ right upper zone.
RVA right visual acuity.
RVH right ventricular hypertrophy.

S

S schedule e.g., S 4 — schedule iv Poisons; single dose; sister.
S 1–5 sacral spinal segments.

SAE stamped addressed envelope.
SAH subarachnoidal haemorrhage.
SARE serum angiotensin converting enzyme.
Sat satisfactory.
SB stillborn.
SBE sub-acute bacterial endocarditis.
SC sub-cutaneous.
SEN State Enrolled Nurse.
SG specific gravity.
SGOT serum glutamic oxaloacetic transaminase.
SGPT serum glutamic pyruvic transaminase.
SH social history.
SI sacro-iliac; schedule 1; soluble insulin; statutory instrument.
Sig signa (Latin) label (in prescriptions).
SLE systemic lupus erythematosus.
SM systolic murmur.
SMO Senior Medical Officer.
SMR sub-mucous resection.
SN student nurse.
Sn Snellen test type.
SNO Senior Nursing Officer.
SOA swelling of ankles.
SOB short of breath.
SOBOE short of breath on exertion.
SOL space-occupying lesion.
SOP surgical outpatients.

SOS supplementary ophthalmic service.

Spec Gr specific gravity.

Spt spirit; sputum.

S(R) single dose — usually repeated 2 or 3 times in the day.

St stone (of weight).

Stat immediately (refers to administration of drugs).

STs sanitary towels.

STD sexually transmitted disease.

Sub subsequent dose.

Sulpha sulphonamide.

SVD simple vertex delivery.

SVT supraventricular tachy-cardia.

SWD short wave diathermy.

Sy syphilis.

Syph syphilis.

T

T temperature; term; treatment.

T 1–12 thoracic spine segments.

TA triple antigen.

T & A tonsils and adenoids.

TAB typhoid-paratyphoid A and B vaccine.

TABC typhoid-paratyphoid A, B and C vaccine.

TAB/Cho typhoid-paratyphoid A + B vaccine + cholera vaccine.

TABT typhoid-paratyphoid A and B vaccine with tetanus toxoid.

TB tuberculosis.

TBM tuberculous meningitis.

TCA3(7) to come again in three (seven) days.

TCI to come in.

Tet tetanus, tetracycline.

Tet/Ser tetanus antitoxin.

Tet/Vac tetanus toxoid.

Tet/VacFT tetanus toxoid.

Th V thoracic vertebra.

TI tricuspid incompetence.

t.i.d. ter in die (Latin) three times a day.

t.d.s. three times a day.

TN temperature normal.

TPI treponemal immobilisation test.

TPR temperature, pulse, respiration.

TPV triple polio vaccine.

TR temporary resident.

TS tricuspid stenosis.

TSH thyroid stimulating hormone.

TT tetanus toxoid; tuberculin tested.

TTA to take away ⎫ refers
TTH to take home ⎬ to
TTO to take out ⎭ drugs

TV trichomonas vaginalis.

U

U unit.

U and E urea and electrolytes.
UG urogenital.
UGS urogenital system.
UGT urogenital tract.
UMN upper motor neurone.
UMT unit of medical time.
URTI upper respiratory tract infection.
U/S ultrasound.
UTI urinary tract infection.
UVL ultra-violet light.

V

V visit.
V 10 visit in 10 days.
VA visual acuity.
Vac vaccination.
Vag vaginitis.
VD venereal disease.
VDRL Venereal Disease Research Laboratory.
VDRT venereal disease reference test.
VE vaginal examination; varicose eczema.
VF ventricular fibrillation.
VI virgo intacta.
VSD ventricular septal defect.
VT ventricular tachycardia.

VU varicose ulcer.
VV varicose vein(s).
Vx vertex.

W

W weekly dose.
WBC white blood cell count; white blood corpuscles.
WC water closet = lavatory; whooping cough.
WR Wassermann reaction.
Wt weight.
WVS Women's Voluntary Service.

X

X multiple.
XR X-ray.
Xs excess.

Y

yr year.

Z

ZA Zondek–Aschheim.
ZN Ziehl–Neelsen.

7 Descriptive language of systems review

When a doctor has taken a history of the patient's complaints, it is customary to enquire whether the patient has complaints of any other system. Patients are not used to talking about their bodily functions and abnormalities and often cannot easily find the precise words to describe the character of pain, the consistency of stool, the tone of cough and so on.

Here are some of the questions that doctors ask repeatedly about urine, stools, sputum etc. and the appropriate words to describe the colour, form and smell. It is difficult for a patient to be specific about the *amount* of blood, sputum and so on lost. A doctor, therefore, often suggests household utensils to give an idea of the measurement: 'How much sputum do you bring up? An egg-cupful?' Be sure you are familiar with the size of teaspoons, dessertspoons, tablespoons, egg-cup, tea-cup, etc.

BLOOD

Blood; to bleed; bleeding.
To lose blood; to have a haemorrhage; loss of blood.

Useful questions

Have you had any loss of blood?
Have you noticed any blood in your motions/in your sputum/when you pass water?

Have you noticed any clots of blood?
Was the blood bright or dark in colour?

Descriptive words

Black; bright/dark; brown; coffee grounds; fresh/stale; heavy/slight loss of blood; pink; watery; sticky; streaky with mucus.
Arterial jetting.
Capillary oozing.
Venous flowing.

Colloquial expressions

On the paper (as a result of piles).
Splash in the pan (from the rectum seen in the lavatory).
Spotting (on the pad — intramenstrual bleeding).

BOWELS

Medical words: faeces, stools, to defaecate.
Colloquial words: motion, to have the bowels opened. See pages 192–193 for examples of other colloquial expressions.

Useful questions

How often do you have your bowels opened?
Is this a life-long habit?
What do the motions look like?
Are they quite well formed?
What about the colour? Has it changed?
Are they darker in colour?
Have you ever seen any blood in your motions?
Have you noticed an unpleasant smell?
Do you ever have diarrhoea or constipation?
Do you have to go in a hurry?
Can you hold your motions?
Do you have to strain to pass your motions? (tenesmus)

Do you take laxatives?
Do the motions float on the water after flushing the lavatory?
Do you ever have any pain on passing your motions?
Do you get pain before, during or after passing your motions?
Do you suffer from wind?
Have you noticed any special food upsets your bowels?
Have you lost any weight?

Descriptive words

Colour: black; brown; clay-like; colourless — like rice-water (cholera); dark brown; green; grey; pale; pea-soup-like; putty-like, porridge-like (steatorrhoea); redcurrant jelly-like; slaty grey; tarry; white; yellow.

Form and consistency: bloody; bulky; dry; fatty; floating; friable; frequent; frothy; greasy; hard; hard dry balls (scybalae); loose; purulent (with pus); slimy (excess of mucus); soft; watery; well-formed; worms.

Amount: copious; scanty.

Odour: offensive — very bad.

BREATHING

Medical words: respiration, expiration, inspiration.
Colloquial words: breathing, breathing out, breathing in.

Useful questions

Have you had any difficulty with your breathing?
Do you get short of breath?
Do you get short of breath when you run for a bus or climb stairs?
Do you get any pain on breathing?
Take a deep breath, hold your breath and then breathe out slowly.

Descriptive words

Breathless; deep; jerky; laboured; noisy; out of breath; puffed; quick;

quiet; rapid; regular/irregular; shallow; shortness of breath; troubled; weak; wheezing.

CARDIOLOGY

Useful questions

Do you ever have palpitations?

Are you ever aware of your heart beating fast?

Do you have any chest discomfort or chest pain?

Does the discomfort appear to be brought on by anything in particular?

Does the chest discomfort, for instance, occur more commonly when you are sitting in a chair or when you are walking?

When you do have your chest discomfort/pain, have you noticed that it is accompanied by anything else?

What do you do when you get your chest pain (or chest discomfort)?

Does position make any difference to your chest discomfort/pain?

Do you ever get chest pain/discomfort at night?

If you take the trinitrin (or tablet under the tongue) how quickly does this help relieve the chest discomfort/pain?

Does the chest discomfort/pain spread anywhere else in the body?

Do you ever become dizzy?

Have you ever fainted?

Before you actually faint, are you aware that you are about to faint?

Do you actually lose consciousness or are you aware of your surroundings and people talking?

Do you actually fall to the ground?

When you feel faint, are you able to steady yourself against the wall or an object?

Do you sometimes feel faint when you get up from a chair or out of a hot bath?

If you have palpitation, how would you first become aware of it?

Does it come on gradually or in some other way?

Are there any other symptoms that you notice when you have palpitation?

When your heart is beating fast can you tell whether it is beating regularly or irregularly?

Could you try beating out the rate and the rhythm for me with your hand?

How long have your ankles been swollen?

Are they swollen first thing in the morning?

How far can you walk?

Can you walk as far as you could five years ago?

How many flights of stairs can you climb?

If I walked with you for half a mile, could you keep up with me?

If you have a fainting episode can you describe the sequence of events leading up to it?

COUGH

Useful questions

How long have you had a cough?

Did anything special bring it on?

What kind of cough is it?

When do you get it?

Does any position make it worse?

Do you bring anything up?

Do you get a pain in your chest when you cough?

Descriptive words

Tone: barking; brassy; hacking; hawking (catarrhal and chronic sinusitis); husky; stridulous; wheezing (bronchitis).

Character: dry/productive, explosive/suppressed; postural/not postural; spasmodic/persistent.

DISCHARGE

A discharge.

To discharge.

Useful questions

How long have you had this discharge from your ear/nose/rectum/vagina?
How often do you get it?
How much is there?
What colour is it?
Does it contain casts, clots, mucus, pus?

Descriptive words

Colour: brownish-yellow; creamy white; green; yellow.
Type: blood-stained; milky; with pus; with serum.
Odour: foetid; offensive.

LOCOMOTOR

Useful questions

Do you have any pain or stiffness in any joints?
Do you have any pain or stiffness in your limbs, your neck or back?
How long does the stiffness last?
Do you have any tingling in the hands or feet?
Is it worse in the morning or evening?
Any swelling?
Are there any movements that you now find difficult?
Does it affect your daily living?
Have you had a skin rash?
Have you noticed a discharge down below?
Have you had any ulcers in your mouth?
Have you noticed any dryness of your mouth or eyes?

MENSTRUATION

To menstruate: to have one's period(s).
See page 193 for examples of other colloquial expressions.

Useful questions

When did your periods first start?
How often do you see/get/have your periods?
How long do they last?
How much do you lose? Are they heavy?
If patient replies 'Yes':
How many pads do you use each day?
Do you wear pads as well as tampons?
Do you ever pass clots? How big are they?
Do you get pain before or during your periods?
How do you feel before your periods start?
Do you feel edgy (nervous) irritable?
Do you get any bleeding after intercourse or between your periods?
When was your last period?

The menopause

See page 201 for examples of colloquial expressions.
Are you still having your periods?
Are they regular?
When did you see the last one?
Do you get hot flushes and sweats? How often?
Do the flushes interrupt your sleep?
Do you have any trouble when you have intercourse?
Do you have soreness or dryness?
Do you have bleeding after intercourse?
Do you have itching?
Have you had any bleeding since your periods stopped?
Have you had any discharge?

NEUROLOGY

Useful questions

Do you suffer from headaches?
Are they worse in the morning or evening?
In which part of the head do you get the pain?

Do you ever feel sick or vomit?
Does the light hurt your eyes?
Any other trouble with your eyes?
Have you noticed any blurring of vision?
Do you ever see things double?
Do you ever see flashing lights?
Have you had any fits, faints or funny turns?
Was there any warning you were going to have a fit?
Did you bite your tongue?
Did you wet yourself?
Do you have any problems with your hearing?
Have you noticed any numbness, tingling or weakness in your limbs?
Are you passing more water than you used to?
Can you control your bowel movements?

OBSTETRICS

To be pregnant: to be expecting a baby.
See pages 193, 194, 201 and 202 for examples of other colloquial expressions.

Useful questions

Is this your first pregnancy?
How many children have you?
How old are they?
How long did your pregnancy last?
Did you have any trouble during pregnancy such as raised blood pressure?
Was labour induced or did it start by itself?
How long were you in labour?
Did you have a normal delivery/forceps/Caesarian operation?
Have you had any miscarriages (spontaneous abortions)?
At what stage of pregnancy were they?

PAIN

Pain and ache mean the same thing and we speak of 'aches and pains' generally. Both these words are nouns but the word 'ache' can be used with the following to form a compound noun:

Backache; earache; headache; stomach-ache; toothache. For the other parts of the body we say, 'I have a pain in my shoulder, chest,' etc.

It is possible to have a pain in the back, head and stomach but this generally refers to a more serious condition than backache, headache and stomach-ache.

The word 'ache' can also be used as a verb: 'My leg aches after walking ten miles.' 'My back aches after gardening.'

The word 'hurt' is another verb used to express injury and pain: 'My chest hurts when I cough.' 'My neck hurts when I turn my head.'

Useful questions

Duration: How long have you had this pain?

Site: Where do you get the pain? Show me exactly where you get the pain.

Character: What kind of pain is it?

Onset: Did it come on slowly or suddenly?

Time: When do you get the pain?

Severity: Does it wake you up at night?

Cause: Does anything special bring it on? (emotional disturbance, exercise, food, position, etc).

Does anything special make it worse?

Radiation: Does it spread anywhere else?

Relief: Does anything relieve it? (Drug, exercise, food, heat, position, rest).

Character:

beating;

biting;

boring;

burning, (as in cystitis, ulcer);

bursting;

colicky (abdominal disease);
crampy;
cutting (rectal disease);
dragging;
drawing;
dull (headache, tumour);
gnawing (tumour), pronounced nawing;
grinding;
griping;
gripping (as in angina pectoris);
heavy (as pre-menstrual);
knife-like;
numb (lack of sensation);
piercing (angina pectoris);
pinching;
pressing;
prickling (like pins and needles in inflamed eyes, conjunctivitis);
scalding (cystitis);
severe pain — gip, 'It gives me the gip';
sharp;
shooting (sciatica, toothache);
sickening;
smarting (burns);
sore;
stabbing (indigestion);
stinging (cuts, stings);
stitch (spasm in side due to excessive exercise);
straining;
tearing;
tender;
throbbing (headache);
tingling (return of circulation to extremities);
twinge (sudden, sharp).

Other words to describe pain: acute/chronic; constant/intermittent;
    localised/diffuse, radiating, spreading; mild/severe; superficial/deep-
    seated; constricting; convulsive, spasmodic; darting, fleeting;
    intense, very severe, violent, agonising, excruciating; persistent,
    obstinate, difficult to move, stubborn.

PSYCHIATRY

Useful questions

How has your mood been lately?
Have you felt sad or depressed?
Have you felt like crying at all?
Have you felt anxious or worried?
Have you felt frightened about anything?
Are you finding it difficult to cope with life at the moment?
Do you get angry more easily than usual?
How've you been sleeping?
Do you have any difficulty falling asleep?
Do you wake up earlier than usual?
Are you eating normally?
Do you have a good appetite?
Are you losing weight?
Are you able to enjoy the things you normally do?
Have you lost interest in things around you?
How do you see the future turning out?
Do you think it's possible for you to get better?
Do you ever feel life isn't worth living any more?
Do you ever think about wanting to die or wishing you were dead?
Do you ever have any thoughts about harming yourself?
Do you ever feel yourself sweating more than usual?
Do you ever feel your heart pounding?
Does your mouth go dry?
Is there anything particular that brings these feelings on?
When you feel tense and anxious, is there anything that makes you feel better?
Have you had any trouble with your nerves?
Do you live with anyone?
Have you anyone you can talk to about your problems?
How long have you been in the same job?
Do you enjoy your work?

Drinking habits (See p. 195 for examples of colloquial expressions)

Do you drink at all?
Do you drink every day or just on social occasions?
Roughly, how much do you drink on average every day?
Do you drink alone?
Do you drink in the mornings?
Have you ever been a drinker?
Do you ever feel guilty about your drinking?
Have you ever tried to cut down your drinking?
Have you ever had any fits or black-outs through drinking?
Do you think your drinking causes any problems? At work? With your marriage?
Have you ever got into trouble with the law through drinking?

PULSE

Useful question

Do you get palpitations?

Descriptive words

Absent; bounding; collapsing; faint; fast; feeble; frequent; full; galloping; hard; intermittent; irregular (a) regularly irregular (extrasystole); (b) irregularly irregular (atrial fibrillation); jerking; low; quick; rapid; regular; slow; small; soft; strong; tensed; thready; vibrating; weak.

SKIN

Useful questions

Do you have any problem with your skin?
Have you ever had a skin rash?
Any itching of the skin?
Do you have any allergies?
Is there eczema or psoriasis in your family?

What medication are you using?
Are you using anything on your skin?

SPUTUM

Medical words: sputum, to expectorate.
Colloquial words: phlegm (pronounced flem), to bring up phlegm.

Useful questions

Do you bring up any phlegm?
How much do you bring up?
When do you bring it up?
What colour is it?
Have you noticed any blood?
Is it frothy, watery, etc?
Is there a lot of blood or just streaky with blood?

Descriptive words

Colour: black-grey; blood-stained; brown; dark red; flecked; green;
   pinkish; prune juice-like; raspberry-like; rusty-brown (pneumonia);
   streaked; yellow.
Quality: clear; frothy; glassy; jelly-like; opaque; presence of cysts,
   bile, pellets, etc.; sticky; thick; thin; transparent.
Odour: foetid; nauseating; putrid.

UROLOGY

Medical words: to micturate, to urinate.
Colloquial words: to pass water. See page 194 for examples of other
   colloquial expressions.

Useful questions

Do you have any difficulty in passing your water?
Is the difficulty when you start passing your water, throughout or
afterwards?

Does your water gush?
Does your water dribble?
Does it come away when you cough, laugh, sneeze or strain?
How often do you pass water?
Do you have to get up in the night (to pass water)?
Has the amount of water you pass increased/decreased?
How much urine do you pass each time?
Have you noticed any change in the colour of your water?
Have you seen any blood in your water?
Do you have any pain when you pass your water?
Does your water burn or sting?
I'd like to have a specimen (sample) of your water.
I'd like to have a mid-stream specimen.

Descriptive words

Colour: amber; black; brown; blood-streaked; blue-green (as result
of drugs for back and kidney); orange; pink; red; reddish-brown;
straw-coloured (normal); yellow.
Character: clear; cloudy; flecked; foaming; frothy; milky; muddy;
thick; transparent; turbid; slimy; smoky.
Odour: ammoniacal; fishy; foetid; fruity and sweet (diabetes).

VOMITING

Medical word: to vomit.
Colloquial words: to be sick, to bring up food. See page 194 for
examples of other colloquial expressions.

Useful questions

How long have you been sick?
Do you feel better after being sick (or after vomiting)?
How often do you vomit?
How much do you vomit?
What colour is the vomit?
Have you noticed any coffee grounds, bile, blood in your vomit?

When do you vomit?
Is it related to eating?
Do you feel sick before you vomit or does it just happen?
Do you retch?

Descriptive words

Colour: black; blood; coffee-grounds; green.
Character: copious; frothy; residues of food; sour-smelling; watery
  fluid.

SENTENCES FOR ALL PARTS OF THE BODY

These sentences cover most parts of the body that your patient will
speak of. Most of the sentences come from case histories, others are
from medical reports. Notice the structure of the sentence and the
use of tenses. From these sentences you can make dozens more by
simply changing the details. Look at these examples:

I've had this *swelling* on my *neck* for *two weeks*.
  lump   breast six weeks
  spot   eyelid three months
  ulcer   tongue five days
When I'm tired, *my eyelid flickers*.
  my head aches
  my back aches
  I can't sleep properly
  I can't eat
By developing this method, you will be sure of making a perfect
English sentence. It will also help you to stop translating from your
own language.

HEAD AND NECK

The man suffered from recurring intense *headaches*.
My *hair* has been dropping out for the past three months.
Since I had shingles, I've had a deadness and tingling feeling in my
forehead.

I keep getting a sharp pain in my *temple*.

When I'm tired, my *eyelid* flickers.

Her eyelashes have grown in the wrong direction. They rub on the *cornea* and cause irritation.

When a patient is jaundiced, *the whites of his eyes* are yellow.

I have a strange creepy feeling on my *scalp*.

The patient had felt generally unwell for some time and then she noticed she had pink spots all over her *face*.

The boy's *pupils* were dilated as a result of drugs.

There is some hard wax in this *ear*. I'll give you some drops to soften it.

I've got terrible catarrh and can't breathe through my *nose*.

I've found I have a lump inside my *mouth* and I'm worried about it.

In winter my *lips* are cracked.

I'm afraid you'll have to have this *tooth* extracted.

When I brush my *teeth*, my *gums* bleed.

In undulant fever (brucellosis, Malta Fever) the *tongue* frequently has a central white fur.

You've come out in a rash all over your *cheek*.

The child fell down and cut open his *chin*. He had to have five stitches in it.

In tetanus, stiffness of the *jaw* occurs until the patient is unable to open his *mouth*.

I've had this swelling on my *neck* for two weeks.

When I eat, I can't swallow properly. It feels as if everything is sticking in my *throat*.

ARMS AND HANDS

The old woman slipped and dislocated her *shoulder*.

I've had pain and swelling under my *arm* (in my *armpit*) for several weeks.

When I play tennis, I get a pain in my *elbow* and it is painful to straighten my *arm*.

Last year I broke my *arm* and had to have it in plaster.

When he was playing cricket, he sprained his *wrist*. It was painful and swollen.

The man who worked with a pneumatic drill said in winter his *hands* were numb and painful.

The girl noticed irritation on the *palm of her hand* and between the *fingers* and it turned out to be scabies.

I was washing the floor and a pin went into my *thumb*. Half of it is broken inside.

My *knuckles* are so swollen when I wake up.

The old man was unable to clench his *fist*.

My *nails* keep on breaking and splitting.

LEGS AND FEET

The man's *leg* was amputated because gangrene set in.

I'm going into hospital next week to have these veins on my *thighs* stripped.

I keep getting a lot of pain in my left *knee*. Sometimes it feels as if it will give way.

The man had severe pain in his *calves* when he was walking. After a short rest the pain went off.

She was walking along when suddenly she felt a severe pain in her *foot*.

The boy sprained his *ankle* playing football. It became blue, swollen and painful.

She had trouble with her *feet*. They were covered with chilblains in winter and she had a bunion on her *big toe* and a *hammer toe*.

My little boy gets swelling and tenderness at the back of his *heel* and it is so painful that he limps.

BODY

I keep getting a stabbing pain in my *chest* and I get out of breath when I go upstairs.

Many women have pain and fullness in their *breast* before their period.

One of the signs of cancer of the breast is *nipple* retraction.

A 34-year-old woman had been found to have a *heart* murmur during her first pregnancy six years previously.

I get a sharp pain in my *side* when I crouch or stand up.

The man fell from a ladder and broke two of his *ribs*.

I've got arthritis in my *hip* and some days I can hardly move.

I get a burning pain and a blown-up feeling in my *stomach*.

I mustn't eat rich food because I've had *gallstones* for years.

I've noticed blood in my motions and I get a pain in my *back passage* (anus).

I'm having a lot of trouble with my *bowels*. Sometimes I'm constipated and then I get diarrhoea.

She had had *bladder* trouble since she was a child.

I'm afraid we shall have to remove the *womb*.

The patient complained of a swelling in the *groin* and a *vaginal* discharge.

I keep wanting to pass water and I have a pain in my *back*. Do you think it's *kidney* trouble, doctor?

I've got a pain in my *private parts (penis)*.

8 Colloquial English

VOCABULARY USED BY PATIENTS TO DISCUSS SYMPTOMS

Many patients find extreme difficulty in discussing their bodily functions and symptoms of disorder with a doctor. This may be from ignorance or shyness. Obviously the more intimate the part of the body, the greater the embarrassment, and so a wide vocabulary of euphemisms and slang expressions has sprung up in the English language. Some of them are used by uneducated people, others by embarrassed educated people.

Quite often the patient is so inarticulate that the doctor has to suggest various symptoms and the patient merely says 'yes' or 'no'. In this case, the doctor often uses colloquial expressions himself which he thinks the patient will understand.

Regional expressions have been mainly excluded in the following chapters. Those phrases which are most commonly used have been printed in italics, for example, *back passage*. Those which are vulgar or low and are not commonly used in polite society, have been marked with an asterisk, *.

PARTS OF THE BODY

Anus: arse*, arsehole*, *back passage*, hole*.

To break wind: to fart*, to poop*, to trump*.

Bladder: waterworks, e.g. Doctor to patient: 'How are the waterworks?'

How is your bladder working?

Bowels: gut, e.g. a pain in one's gut, to have belly ache (often used to mean bowels), to have gut ache.

Brain: head-piece.

Breast: boobs*, *bosom*, buffers*, *bust*, charleys*, *chest*, chestnut*, globe*, knockers*, nipples, paps*, tits*, titties*, top part.

Imitation breasts: falsies.

Buttocks: arse*, backside*, *behind, bottom*, botty (childish), bum*, cheeks, hind quarters, posterior, rear, rump*, *seat, sit-me-down* (nursery), sit-upon, stern, tail, toby.

To have large buttocks: to be broad in the beam.

Cervix: neck of womb.

Chest: to have a *flat*, barrel, *hollow*, pigeon chest.

The following are only used for females:

bosom, breast, buffers*, *bust*.

To have a bad cough: *to bark*.

Coughing: *to be chesty, a bit chesty*.

To have one's chest finger-tapped: to have a thump.

Clitoris: clit*.

Crotch: often used to mean groin or skin covering genitalia.

Ear: bat ears (prominent), a cauliflower ear (from boxing), flappers, lug*, (e.g. to have lugache*).

Rather deaf: to be hard of hearing.

Elbow: *funny bone*, e.g. *to hit one's funny bone* (so called because of the strange tingling one experiences when it is struck).

Eyes: glimmers*, ogles*, optics, peepers.

To have a squint: to be boss-eyed, to be cock-eyed, to be wall-eyed.

To have low visual acuity in one eye: to have a lazy eye.

Face: clock*, dial*, mug*, physog*.

Genitals: male and female-affair, *down below, private parts*, thing, pencil and tassle* (male child's penis and scrotum), twig and berries* (male child's penis and testicles).

Hand: mitt, paw.

Head: bonce; brain-box, brain-pan, napper, nob, noddle, nous-box (nous means intelligence, common sense), nut, *skull*.

Heart: engine, e.g. 'my engine's not working properly', jam tart* (Cockney), *ticker*.

Something wrong with one's heart: to have a cardiac heart, *to have a dicky heart*.

To have a weak heart: to have a heart.

Hymen: maidenhead, maid's ring (Cockney).

Intestines: bowels, guts, innards, *inside*.

Legs: bandy legged (bow), drumsticks (very thin), K-legged (with knees knocking together), knock-kneed (knees bent inwards to face each other), peg leg (a wooden leg), pins, spindles.

A lame leg: to have a gammy leg.

Short legs: to have duck's disease.

Walk badly: to be bad on one's pins.

Walking with the feet turned in: hen-toed.

Lungs: bellows, tubes.

To be bad in one's breathing: *to be short-winded*.

Mouth: chops*, gob* trap*.

Navel: belly button.

Neck: Adam's apple (projection of thyroid cartilage of larynx), salt cellars (very deep hollows above collar-bone in female neck), scruff of neck (nape).

Nose: beacon* (red and large), beak*, conk*, hooter*, sniffer*, snitch*.

Nasal congestion: to be blocked up, bunged up, *stuffy*.

Nasal discharge: snot*.

Noisy breathing in children due to nasal congestion: snuffles.

Running nose: a snotty nose*.

Penis: almond*, almond rock* (Cockney), bean*, button* (baby), club*, cock*, dick*, equipment*, gear*, it*, John Thomas*, knob*, little man*, little tail* (small boys), meat*, old man*, Peter*, pinkle*, prick*, *private parts*, privates, shaft*, she*, stick*, tadger* (Northern England), tassel*, thing*, tool*, Will*, Willie*.

Scrotum: bag*.

Skull: brain pan.

Spine: backbone.

Stomach: abdomen, belly, bread-basket*, corporation (when large), croop, guts (stomach and intestines), innards, inner man, peenie, pinafore, *tummy*.

To belch: *to burp*.

The noise the stomach makes when one is hungry: *to have stomach rumbles*.

Something wrong with it: to have a gastric stomach.

Stomach ache: to have a pain in one's guts.

Distension of stomach in older people: middle age spread.

Teeth: buck teeth (protruding); peggy, peggies (nursery talk).

Testicles: ballocks*, bollocks*, balls*, charleys*, cobblers*, cods*, nuts*, pills*, pillocks*, stones*. See **Genitals.**

Throat: clack*, gullet, organ-pipe (wind-pipe).

A very severe cough: a churchyard cough.

Sputum: *phlegm*.

To be hoarse: *to have a frog in the throat*.

To have a sore throat: to have a throat.

Tongue: clack*, clapper*.

The tongue can be described as: coated, dirty, *furred*, furry, thick.

Talkative person: *a chatterbox*.

Trachea: *windpipe*.

Urethra: pipe.

Vagina (or vulva): birth canal, box*, brush*, crack*, cunt*, *down below*, fanny*, *front passage*, hairpie*, it, private, e.g. 'my private is sore', *private part*, pubes*, pussy*, slit*, thing*, there, twat*, up inside.

Umbilicus: *navel*.

Uterus: box, *womb*.

BODILY FUNCTIONS

Defaecate, to: to crap*, to do a big job, to do a job, to do a pooh (childish), to do a rear*, to do number two, to do one's business, to do one's duty, to go to the ground*, to go to the toilet (and use paper), to have a clear out, *to have the bowels opened*, to job*, to shit*, *to use a bedpan* (hospital).

Faeces, stools: baby's yellow (infantile excrement), business, cack*, job*, mess*, *motions*, number two, shit*.

Doctor to patient: 'Are your motions well formed?'

Mothers often say of a child: 'His toilet is green.' (Meaning his stools are green.)

Note that 'a dose of salts', means Epsom salts.

Tenesmus: *straining*.

Constipation, to have: to be costive, *I haven't been for four days.* I haven't had a road through me for a week*.

Diarrhoea, to have: back door trots*, collywobbles, Gippy tummy, run'ems, runs, scours, skitters*, squitters*.

To have a sudden attack of diarrhoea: *to be taken short.*

Die, to: to be a goner, to be all over, to be slipping (to be dying), to burn oneself out (die early through overwork), to conk out, to go (go away), to go home, to go to the next world, to hang up one's hat, to have had it, to have one's number up, to have had one's chips, to have one foot in the grave (to be dying), to kick the bucket, *to pass away*, to peg out, to pip out, to pop off (usually die suddenly), to push up daisies, to snuff it or out, to turn it in, to turn one's toes up, *to have had a long* (or *good*) *innings* (to die at an old age), *to lay out* (prepare for burial).

Note: to commit suicide: to kill oneself.

Faint, to: *to black out, to have a black-out*, to go off hooks, to pass out.

Impotent, to become: to be no good to one's wife, to lose one's nature.

A man's impotence will be expressed by his wife in the following ways: he can't sustain an erection, *he can't manage*, his cock's soft or droopy*.

Menstruate, to: to be indisposed, to be on the rag*, to be unwell, to have a visitor, one's monthly, *one's period*, colours, *the curse*, the flux, the days, the other, the plague, the poorlies, the rags up*, the thing, *the time of the month*, the usual.

'Have you seen anything?' (feminine euphemism).

'I haven't seen for six weeks' (no menstruation, probably pregnant).

Doctor to patient: 'When was your last period?'

Naked, to be: to be in one's birthday suit, to be in the altogether, to be starkers.

Pregnant, to be: away the trip* (Scottish working class), to be caught*, *to be expecting, to be having a baby*, to be in a delicate condition, to be in an interesting condition, to be in Kittle (Scottish), to be in pig*, to be in pod*, to be in the club*, to be in the family way, to be in the pudding club*, to be one in line*, to be preggers*, to be up the pole*, to be up the stick*, to catch on, to catch the virus*, to click*, to cop it*, to fall for a baby (to have an unwanted pregnancy), to have a bun in the oven*, to have a touch of the sun*.

She's six months pregnant: she's six months gone. (See pages 201–202 for further examples.)

Fluttering sensation felt by woman when pregnant: quickening.

Sleep, to: to close one's eyes, *to doze* (short sleep), *to go off* (to fall asleep), to go to the land of nod, *to have a cat-nap* (short sleep), *to have a doze*, *to have a snooze* (short sleep), *to have forty winks* (short sleep), *to have some shut-eye*, *to nod off* (short sleep), ziz.

Urinate, to (micturate): to do number one, to go round the corner, to go to see a man about a dog, to go to see one's aunt, to have a run-out, *to pass water*, to pee, to pee-wee (childish), to piddle*, to piss*, *to spend a penny* (women only), to tiddle (childish), to tinkle (women only), to wee-wee (childish).

Expressions:

Nocturia: to get up in the night.

Hostess to guests: 'Do you want to wash your hands?' (do you want to go to the toilet?).

The lavatory can be described as: *bathroom*, bog*, *cloakroom*, convenience, *Gents'*, heads*, *Ladies'*, lav., lavvy, little girls' room, *loo*, place, powder room (Ladies' in a hotel), privies, rears*, *toilet*, W.C.

A chamber pot: banjo*, gerry*, po, pot, potty (childish).

To hold a baby over a chamber pot: to hold out a baby.

To put a baby on a chamber pot: to pot.

Vomit, to: to be ill, *to be sick*, to bring up, to lose the lot, to puke*, to pump your heart up, to sick up, to spew*, to throw up*.

Nausea: the sicks.

To have nausea: to feel queasy, *to feel sick*.

'Have you vomited?' '*Have you been sick?*'

To try to vomit but nothing comes up: *to retch*.

To vomit very much: to be as sick as a dog (or cat).

To have a headache and vomiting: to have a sick headache.

Weep to: to blub, to blubber, to break down, *to cry*, to turn on the waterworks, to turn the tap on.

MENTAL AND PHYSICAL STATES

Angry, to be: to be cross, to be crusty, to be heated, to be hot under the collar, to be liverish, to be livid, to be shirty, to be steamed up, to fly off the handle, to go off the deep end, to have a paddy, to have a tantrum, to jump down someone's throat, to let off steam, to lose one's hair, to lose one's shirt, to play the devil, to see red.

Depressed, to be: to be blue, to be browned-off, to be down in the hips, to be down in the mouth, to be fed up, to be in the dumps, to be low, to be off the hinges, to have a button on, to have a chopper, to have a face as long as a fiddle, to have the droops, to have the hump, to have the hyp, to have the mopes, to have the pip.

Drunk, to be: to be a dipso (dipsomaniac), to be boozed (boozy), to be fou*, to be fresh (slightly drunk), to be fuddled (confused with drink), to be high, to be high on surge (to be drunk on surgical spirit), to be lush (slightly drunk), to be merry (happy with drink), to be muzzed, to be on the bottle (habitual drinker), to be plastered, to be paralytic (very drunk), to be slewed, to be sloshed, to be soaked (very drunk), to be sozzled (very drunk), to be squiffy (slightly drunk), to be stoned (very drunk), to be tiddly (slightly drunk), to be tight, to be tipsy (slightly drunk), to be under the influence (of liquor), to be well-oiled, to be woozy (confused with drink), to have a skinful (very drunk), to have Dutch courage (extra courage induced by drink), to have more than one can carry, to have one over the eight, to see pink elephants (or spiders) (to suffer from DTs), to have a hang-over (to feel ill as a result of drink), to have a morning-after-the-night-before (to feel ill as a result of drink), to hit the bottle (to drink excessively).

Dull, to be: to be a dream, a drip, a moron, a muggins, a noodle, a pie-can, a sap*, a wet, dead alive, dopey, dumb, foolish, goofy, half-baked, half-witted, lethargic, mutton-headed, silly, simple, slack, slow, soft, stupid, thick, thick-skulled.

Exhausted, to be: to be all in, to be clapped out*, to be dead, to be done in, for, up, to be fagged out, to be finished, to be flaked out, to be jiggered, to be knackered*, to be knocked up, to be ready to drop, to be shagged*, to be shattered, *to be tired out*, to be used up (utterly exhausted), *to be weary*, to be whacked, to feel like death, to go all to pieces (collapse from exhaustion).

To knock it out of one, '*walking uphill knocks it out of me*' (walking uphill exhausts me).

Healthy, to be: to be A1, to be as fit as a box of birds, to be as fit as a fiddle, to be fighting fit, to be first rate, to be full of beans, to be in fine fettle, to be in the pink, to be on good form, to have plenty of pep (pep = energy), to have plenty of vim (energy, vigour), to perk up (recover good health).

To begin to recover after an illness: *to be on the mend*, to turn the corner.

Madness: (in varying degrees): to be a bit touched, to be a case, to be a character (to be eccentric, odd), a scatterbrain (very forgetful, vague), to be as mad as a hatter, balmy, (barmy), batty, bats, bonkers, to be clean gone, cracked, crackers, crack-pot, crank, crazy, to be dippy, dotty, gaga (senile decay), goofy, half-baked, kinky, loony, loopy, mad, to be MD (mentally deficient), to be mental, non compos mentis, not all there, to be not right in one's head, nuts, off one's block, off one's chump, off one's head, off one's nut, off one's rocker, to be off the rails, out of one's mind, to be peculiar, potty, round the bend, scatty, screwy, a screwball, silly, simple, soft, stupid, up the creek, weak in the upper storey, to go doolally, to go hay-wire, to have bats in the belfry, with a tile (or screw) missing (or loose).

Mental hospital: bin, funny farm, loony bin, nuthouse.

To threaten to lock someone up as a madman: to put in a strait jacket.

Nervous, to feel: to be a fuss-pot, to be a jitter-bug, to be all hot and bothered, to be all of a dither, to be chewed up, *to be edgy*, on edge, to be fidgety, to be in a blue funk, to be in a flap, to be in a stew, to be in a tizzy, to be jittery, to be screwed up, to be shook-up (nerve-racked), to get all het-up, *to get in a state*, to get uptight, to go all hot and cold, to go into a flat spin, to go to pieces (collapse through nerves), to go up the wall, to have ants in one's pants*, to have butterflies in one's stomach, to have forty fits, to have kittens, to have the creeps, to have the heebie-jeebies, to have the shakes, to have the shivers, to have the twitters, to have the willies, to have the wind up, to have the worrits, to worrit (be anxious).

Unwell, to be: to be anyhow, to be below par, to be C$_3$ (very unfit), to be groggy, to be not oneself, to be not quite right, *to be off colour*, to be out of sorts, to be peaky, to be pingley, to be poorly, *to be run down*, to be taken bad, to be tenpence to the bob, *to be under the weather*, to be washed-out, to be weedy (anaemic, sickly), to be wobbly (weak after an illness), to be wonky (weak), to come all over queer, faint, ill (suddenly feel unwell), to crack up, to feel a bit off it, to feel a bit rough, to feel funny, to feel half-baked, to feel like death warmed up (very unwell), to feel like nothing on earth, to feel lousy, to feel queer, to feel ragged, to feel seedy, to have a bad turn.

Vertigo: *to be dizzy*, to be giddy, to be muzzy, to feel the room spin, to feel queer, to have a mazy bout, to have a swimming head.

DISEASES AND OTHER CONDITIONS

Medical name	*Colloquial name*
Alopecia:	baldness.
Angina pectoris:	angina.
Arteriosclerosis:	hardening of the arteries.
Brucellosis:	undulant fever.
Bursitis:	housemaid's knee.
Cancer	a growth
Candida	thrush
Cerebral concussion:	to be concussed, to be knocked out.
Cerebral palsy:	to be spastic.
Cerebral embolism, haemorrhage or thrombosis:	apoplexy, seizure, stroke.
Chorea:	St Vitus' dance.
Colic:	gripes.
Conjunctivitis:	pink eye.
Convulsions:	fits.
Coronary thrombosis; myocardial infarction:	a coronary, heart attack.

Medical name	*Colloquial name*
Contusion:	bruise.
Coryza:	cold in the head.
Dandruff:	scurf.
Delirium tremens:	DTs, the jerks, the shakes.
Diabetes mellitus:	sugar.
Dysmenorrhoea:	painful periods.
Dyspnoea:	breathless, out of breath, puffed, short of breath.
Dyspepsia:	indigestion.
Epilepsy:	fits, the shakes.
Encephalitis:	brain fever.
Encephalitis lethargica:	sleepy sickness.
Enuresis:	bed-wetting.
Erythema pernio:	chilblains.
Flatulence, flatus:	wind, Note: to belch (to send out wind from stomach noisily), to fart* (to send out wind from anus).
Frequency:	I keep wanting to go (to pass urine).
Furuncle:	boil.
Haemorrhoids:	piles.
Halitosis:	bad breath.
Hernia:	rupture.
Herpes simplex:	cold blister or sore.
Herpes zoster:	shingles.
Hordeolum:	stye.
Hydrops:	dropsy.
Hydrophobia:	rabies.
Incontinence:	leaky, not to be able to hold one's water or motions.
Infectious mononucleosis:	glandular fever.
Infective hepatitis:	catarrhal jaundice.
Influenza:	'flu.
Leucorrhoea:	whites.
Luxation:	dislocation, to put out a joint.
Lymphadenoma:	Hodgkin's disease.

Medical name	*Colloquial name*
Menopause:	the change (of life); the turn (of life).
Myopia:	short-sight.
Nephritis:	Bright's disease.
Neuralgia:	face ache.
Nocturia:	to get up at night (to pass water).
Oedema:	dropsy, swelling.
Monilia:	thrush.
Parotitis (viral):	mumps.
Peritonsillar abscess:	quinsy.
Pertussis:	whooping cough.
Poliomyelitis:	infantile paralysis; polio.
Pruritus:	itching.
Pyrexia:	fever, a temperature.
Pyrosis:	heartburn, water-brash.
Raynaud's disease:	white or dead fingers.
Recurrent appendicitis:	grumbling appendix.
Rheumatism:	screws, springes, rheumatics.
Rubella:	German measles.
Rubeola; morbilli:	measles.
Scabies:	the itch.
Scarlatina:	scarlet fever.
Strabismus:	squinting.
Syncope:	fainting.
Tachycardia:	palpitations.
Tetanus:	lockjaw.
Tinea circinata:	ringworm.
Tinnitus:	ringing in the ears.
Tuberculosis:	consumption; TB.
Urticaria:	hives, heat spots; nettlerash.
Varicella:	chickenpox.
Variola:	smallpox.
Verrucae:	warts.
Venous thrombosis:	white leg (in pregnancy).
Vesicle:	blister.

MEDICINE

(In this section the text in bold type is the colloquial expression)

Capsules: unpleasant drugs contained in a soluble case.

Dope, physic: any kind of medicine.

Medicine: anything taken to relieve pain or symptoms of illness. Usually the word refers to liquid or drugs taken by mouth.

Pills, tablets: drugs in tablet form. Note: to be on the pill: to be taking the contraceptive pill.

A tonic: medicine to invigorate one after an illness.

To be at death's door, to be critical, to be nearly a goner: to be dangerously ill.

To be laid up: to be confined to bed, e.g. 'I was laid up for three months.'

To be looking up: to improve.

To be off sick, to be on the sick-list: to be absent from work due to illness.

To be on the mend: to improve.

To be nesh, to be soft: to be prone to illness.

To be under a doctor: to be in a doctor's care.

To find one's legs: to begin to walk after an illness.

To get a chit from the doctor: to get a medical certificate.

To go under: to have an anaesthetic.

To have a bad turn: to become ill suddenly.

To have a bottle: to have a bottle of medicine, e.g. 'Can you give me a bottle for my stomach, doctor?'

To have a bug, a germ: to catch a virus.

To have a check-up: to be medically examined.

To have a set-back: to have a relapse.

To have a temperature: to be feverish, to have a high temperature, e.g. 'I've had a temperature all day'.

To have gas: to have an anaesthetic.

To have painkillers: to have analgesics.

To have sleeping pills: to have sedatives.

To have time off: to have sick leave.

To stitch: to suture.

To suck lozenges: to suck small tablets, usually for coughs and sore throat.

To take a turn for the better: to improve.

To take medicine for the bowels: to take an aperient (the patient uses the word laxative most).

To take stitches out: to remove sutures.

To turn the corner: to improve.

REPRODUCTIVE ORGANS AND SEXUAL PROBLEMS

Gynaecology

The vocabulary to express menstruation and pregnancy is listed separately under Bodily Functions on pages 193–194.

Dilatation and curettage: *D & C*, a scrape, 'I've had two D & Cs' (two scrapes).

Dysmenorrhoea: period pains, to be unwell.

Flooding: excessive bleeding from womb during menopause (or miscarriage).

Hot flushes, to have: to have a high temperature and red face owing to the menopause.

Hysterectomy: to have an internal operation, to have a major operation, to have all taken away (uterus and ovaries).

Menarche: the beginning of periods, e.g. 'When did your periods start?'

Menopause: the end of periods, e.g. 'When did your periods end?', the change, that certain age, the time of life.

I haven't seen anything for 6 months.

It's your age. It's the time of life.

Repair of the prolapse: 'I was stitched up below', to be hitched up.

Sanitary towels: Bunnies, jam rags*, pads, rag*, *STs*.

Vaginal discharge: to have whites, to lose, 'Something comes away from me.'

Obstetrics

Confinement: childbirth, delivery. 'Did you have an easy confinement?'

Episiotomy: to make a cut. 'I'm going to cut you now.'

Parturition: labour, to be in labour. 'How often are you having pains?'

Placenta: the afterbirth.

Rupture the membranes, to: to break the waters.

Still-born baby: baby born dead.

Suture: to be stitched up.

Version: turning (of fetus).

Termination of pregnancy

Abortion: spontaneous miscarriage, a miscarriage, a miss*. 'It came away.' 'I lost my baby.'

Medical termination of pregnancy: an abortion. 'I don't want this baby. Can I have an abortion?'

Efforts to terminate a pregnancy: to bring on a period, to lose it (a baby), to get rid of a baby, to slink*. 'They took the baby away.'

SEXUAL EXPRESSIONS

Anal intercourse: buggery, bumming*.

Dyspareunia: *love pain.*

A French kiss: kiss with mouth open and insert tongue in partner's mouth.

Illegitimate, to be: to be a bastard, to be born on the wrong side of the blanket, to get into trouble (unmarried pregnancy), to have a natural child.

Oral sex: blow job*, fellatio, give head*, sixty-nine* (mutual oral sex), to suck off.

Orgasm: climax.

> To experience an orgasm: *to come*, to have a thrill.
> 'When I come.'
> 'When he's finished.'

Sexual intercourse: intimacy, to do it, to fuck*, to get it with, to get layed, to go with someone, *to go to bed with someone*, to have it, to knock up*, *to make love*, to perform, to screw*, *to sleep with*.

To masturbate: to bring oneself off*, to fiddle*, to jack off*, to jerk off*, to rub up*, to shag*, to shake*, to toss*, to wank*, (wanker: masturbator).

To neck: hug and kiss intimately.

To pet: kiss and caress extensively.

Sexual intercourse is often referred to as *a normal married life* by older people. Note the negative use, such as 'We can't have a normal married life'. Also 'He doesn't trouble me', meaning the husband does not demand sexual intercourse if the wife doesn't want it. 'He doesn't bother about that sort of thing' implies a not very demanding husband. 'He wants it too often' means a demanding one.

Phrases such as, '*When I go with my husband*,' '*When we have it*,' '*When we have sex*,' 'When he does it' are most commonly used by ordinary people.

Male expressions

Coitus interruptus: *to be careful*, to withdraw. 'My husband's very careful.'

Ejaculate, to: to come, to get your rocks off*, to shoot.

Erection, to have an: to have a hard on*, to have a stand*, to have a stiff*, to have the horn*.

Impotent, to be: to have a half-stand*.

Impotent, to become: to lose one's nature.

SEXUAL RELATIONS

To have a regular sexual partner: to go steady.

Homo and hetero-sexual: AC – DC* to be double-jointed*.

Male homosexual: to be a cissy, a dandy, a fag*, a faggot*, a fairy*, a nancy-boy, a pansy, a pouf, a poufter*, a queen, a *queer*, *gay*, kinky.

Homosexual expressions: to be the active/passive partner, eating ass*, reaming*, tonguing (using the mouth on anus), finger fucking*, fisting* (using finger/fist in anus).

Female homosexual/lesbian: to be gay, kinky, to be butch (a lesbian with male characteristics), a dyke, a lessie.

FAMILY PLANNING

Contraceptives

Condom: briefs (short condoms), Durex (trade name often used as a synonym), envelope, French letter, Johnny*, jolly bag*, noddy*, rubber*, sheath, skin.
Diaphragm: Dutch cap, cap.
Intrauterine contraceptive devices (IUCDs): the coil.
Oral contraceptive: the pill.

FERTILITY CLINIC

Doctor: '*How often do you try for a baby?*' When and how often do you have intercourse?
Tubal insufflation: *I had my tubes blown.*
Seminal fluid: your husband's fluid.

VENEREAL DISEASE (VD)

Gonorrhoea: clap, gleet, morning drop, strain, tear, a dose, the whites, to catch a cold.
Monilia: Thrush.
Primary syphilis: bumps (West Indian).
Syphilis: bad blood, lues, siff, pox.
Expressions:
   To have a double event (syphilis and gonorrhoea).
   To piss pins and needles*.
   Scalded (infected with gonorrhoea).
Expressions used by patients:
   I've picked up something.
   I'm afraid I've got it.
   I've caught (or got) something.
   I've got a dose (gonorrhoea).
   I've got a full house* (syphilis and gonorrhoea).
   I've got trouble down below.
   I've noticed something odd.
   I've got trouble with my meat*.

I've been after the girls (or men).

Lice in pubic hair: to be chatty*, to have crabs*.

Note: 'The whites' may be used by women to mean any white vaginal discharge.

West Indians use 'scratch' for irritate or itch, i.e. 'it scratches me' means 'it irritates and I want to scratch'.

Prostitutes may say, 'I'm a business girl,' 'I'm on the game.'

The doctor in a VD clinic will ask: *Have you any discharge? Does it irritate? Do you have pain when you pass water? Have you any swelling? Have you a sore place? Have you a rash?*

Abbreviations used

FTAT   Fluorescent Treponemal Antibody Test.
STS   Serum Test for Syphilis.
TPI   Treponemal Immobilization Test.
VDRL   Venereal Disease Research Laboratory.
VDRT   Venereal Disease Reference Test.

9 Phrasal verbs

Learners of the English language have great difficulty in understanding and using phrasal verbs correctly. That is why a whole chapter of this book is given to them. It is impossible to follow everyday speech without a knowledge of phrasal verbs because we use them in preference to more formal words. To take some simple examples. We talk about 'getting up' in the morning and 'putting our clothes on' rather than rising and dressing. Doctors must use language easily understood by their patients so they ask, for example, 'When did the pain first come on?' meaning onset of pain, or say 'I want you to cut down on fatty foods' meaning reduce intake.

A phrasal verb consists of two (sometimes three) parts: a verb followed by a preposition or adverbial particle. The most commonly used phrasal verbs are formed from the shortest and simplest verbs like come, do, get, go, make and put. It is important to consider the two parts together for the combination often makes a different meaning. Some phrasal verbs can have several meanings.

Many of you reading this book will be working alone so to help you learn these special verbs, test papers follow every section. There are three types of questions:

Type A requires recognition of the phrasal verb before an answer can be given, for example: 'How long was it before the man came round?' In this sentence 'came round' means to regain consciousness so a suitable answer would be: 'Three hours'.

Type B requires recall of the phrasal verb. 'He never regained consciousness after the fall.' Give an expression with come. Answer:

came round. Or you may be asked to complete the sentence: He should have . . . . . . by now from the anaesthetic. Answer: come round.

Type C is an open-ended question and many answers are possible. A model answer is given: Where was the man when he came round? Possible answer: In the bathroom, on the ward, in the Intensive Care Unit, etc.

This list of phrasal verbs is by no means complete. The ones selected are those most frequently heard in the doctor-patient relationship and many of the examples are taken from authentic case histories. The answers to the tests are on pages 236–240.

BREAK

Break down: *(a) collapse mentally or physically, often due to stress.* Dr Foster worked night and day and eventually his health broke down.

(b) cry with grief, shock, etc. When she heard she had to have her leg amputated, she broke down.

(c) fail to work because of electrical, mechanical, etc. fault. The cardiac imaging system has broken down.

(d) fail, discontinue. Negotiations over the ambulance workers' pay dispute have broken down.

Break in: *enter somewhere by force.* I could never sleep alone in the house after burglars broke in.

Break out: *sudden start of disease, fire, violence, war.* An epidemic of cholera broke out in the refugee camp.

Break out in something: *suddenly become covered in.* (i) Whenever I use make-up I break out in a rash. (ii) I keep waking up and breaking out in a cold sweat.

Break through: *make a major discovery or advance.* The medical profession hope to break through in the struggle against AIDS.

Break up: *(a) come to end (of school terms).* When do you break up for Christmas?

(b) deteriorate (of health). He's breaking up under the strain of nursing his wife.

Break something up: *come to end (of relationships).* I've been ill ever since my marriage broke up.

Break with: *end relations with someone.* My son has broken with us since he mixed with this group.

Test

1. Why did the woman break down? (Give a suitable answer.)
2. What has happened to the cardiac imaging system? (Give a reply using an expression with *break*.)
3. Why are you vaccinating these people? (Give a reply using an expression with *break*.)
4. What happens when you use make-up? (Give a suitable reply with *break*.)
5. What caused his health to break up? (Give a suitable reply.)

BRING

Bring something about: *cause something to happen.* Drug abuse brought about his death.

Bring something back: *call to mind.* Talking to you brings back memories of my childhood.

Bring someone back to something: *restore.* A complete change will bring you back to health.

Bring someone down: *defeat, degrade.* Heavy drinking brought him down.

Bring something down: *lower, reduce.* We've managed to bring his temperature down.

Bring something in: *introduce legislation.* The new Health Act they have brought in will mean radical changes.

Bring something on: *cause.* Have you noticed any particular food brings the headaches on?

Bring someone round: *restore to consciousness.* Many fainted in the crush but the ambulancemen brought them round.

Bring someone through: *save someone's life.* Her husband was critically ill but the doctors and nurses struggled all night to bring him through and he survived.

Bring someone to: *restore to consciousness.*

Bring someone up: *rear, teach a child social habits* (often used in passive). His mother died when he was two so he was brought up by his grandmother. (Note: to be well brought up. To be badly brought up.)

Bring something up: *(a) vomit.* She's not well. She brought up her lunch today.
(b) eructation. Do you bring any wind up?

Test

1. What brought him down? (Give a suitable reply.)
2. Do you think eating this will . . . . . . another allergic attack?
3. We are trying to bring down his temperature. (Give another word for *bring down*.)
4. What do you do to an unconscious patient? (Give a reply with *bring*.)
5. Who brought you up? (Give a suitable reply.)

COME

Come about: *happen.* How did the accident come about? He crashed his car in the fog.

Come across: *make an impression of a particular kind.* She comes across as a very nervous woman.

Come across someone/something: *find, meet or see unexpectedly.* I've never come across such a bad case of shingles before.

Come along: *make progress.* You're coming along nicely. We should have those stitches out soon.

Come back: *return.* (i) Make an appointment to come back in a month. (ii) Sometimes I feel fine and then the pain comes back.

Come back to someone: *return to memory.* Yes, what happened is all coming back to me now. I remember falling down the steps.

Come by something: *get, obtain.* How did you come by that scar on your cheek? I was in a fight and someone threw a bottle at me.

Come down (of prices, temperature, etc.): *be lowered, fall.* Your blood pressure has come down since I last saw you.

Come down on someone: *criticise someone, punish.* The police come down heavily on people found with hard drugs.

Come down with something: *become ill with something.* She came down with flu and was unable to keep her appointment.

Come forward: *present oneself, with help, information, etc.* 'Will anyone who saw the accident please come forward?

Come from: *have as one's birthplace or place of residence* (not used in the continuous tenses). Where do you come from? India.

Come in: *(a) be admitted to hospital.* I'd like your mother to come in so we can do one or two tests.
(b) become fashionable, begin to be used. Inhalational anaesthesia came in about the middle of the nineteenth century.

Come off something: *fall from a bicycle, horse, etc.* My son came off his bike and he can't walk properly.

Come on: *(a) encourage someone to hurry, make an effort, try harder* (used in imperative only). Come on Mr Hopkins. Let's see you walk across the room now.
(b) grow, make progress. Good. Your baby's coming on very well.
(c) start (of symptoms, weather, etc.) These dizzy spells come on after lying down if I get up quickly.

Come out: *(a) be published.* When's your new book coming out?
(b) become known. It's just come out that they are closing down the factory and I shall lose my job.
(c) stop work, strike. Do you think doctors and nurses should come out for better working conditions?

Come out in something: *be partially covered in rash, spots, etc.* Her hands came out in a rash after she used a new detergent.

Come over: *begin to feel dizzy, faint, etc.* It's happened twice now travelling home from work. I came over faint.

Come round: *regain consciousness.* Your son hasn't come round yet from the anaesthetic.

Come through something: *recover from a serious illness, accident, survive.* You're lucky to have come through such a terrible accident.

Come to: *regain consciousness.* When I came to, I was on the bathroom floor.

Come under something: *be classified as.* Heroin and cocaine come under Schedule 2 of the Misuse of Drugs Regulations.

Come up: *(a) arise (of a subject).* The question of the rights of patients is always coming up these days.
(b) happen, occur. I'm afraid I shall be late for my clinic. Something urgent has come up.

Test

1. I've never come . . . such a nervous person.
2. Give two phrasal verbs with *come* that mean make progress.
3. It's all coming back to me now. (What does this mean?)
4. Your blood pressure has come . . . . .
5. We appeal to anyone who saw the accident to come forward. (What does this mean?)
6. Why do you want my mother to come in? (Give a suitable reply.)
7. When did the pain first come on? (Give a suitable reply.)
8. How long was it before you came round? (Give another expression for 'came round'.)

CUT

Cut back something: *reduce.* Because of inflation, all departments have had to cut back expenditure drastically.

Cut something down; cut down (on something): *reduce amount or quantity.* (i) I've already cut my cigarettes down to 10 a day. (ii) You must cut down on the fats you eat.

Cut someone off: *break the connection on the telephone* (often used in passive). How annoying. I've just been cut off in the middle of a conversation.

Cut something off: *(a) amputate, remove.* Following the explosion, the man had to have his left leg cut off.
(b) stop the supply of something (often used in passive). The electricity has been cut off.

Cut off: *isolated.* She feels very cut off living in the country.

Cut out something: *(a) excise.* I had this lump on my neck cut out.
(b) stop eating, using. We're being told to cut out salt in our diet.

Cut someone up: *upset emotionally* (usually in the passive). He was terribly cut up by his wife's death.

Test

1. Did the doctor tell you to cut down on anything? (Give a suitable reply.)
2. Please don't cut me . . . . I haven't finished speaking.
3. Give the colloquial expression for 'to amputate.'
4. You must cut out all sweet food from your diet. (What does this mean?)
5. How did he feel when his wife died? (Give a reply with *cut*.)

DO

Do away with oneself: *to commit suicide, kill oneself.* I feel so depressed, Doctor, I could do away with myself.

Do someone in: *(a) exhaust* (usually in passive). At the end of the week I'm absolutely done in.
(b) kill (usually in passive). The old man was done in. (slang)

Do something in: *injure a part of the body.* He did his back in moving furniture.

Do something to something: *cause something to happen* (usually with questions with *what.*) What have you done to your leg? It's bleeding.

Do something up: *(a) fasten with buttons or zip, etc.* Well, Mr Cox, let's see if you can do up your clothes.
(b) modernise, redecorate, restore. These wards are depressing. They need doing up.

Do with something: *(a) be concerned with, connected with* (use with *have to*). His job has something to do with medical ethics.
(b) need, wish for (used with *can* and *could*). You could do with some new glasses. Go and have your eyes tested.

Do without someone/something: *manage without.* We've had to do without a speech therapist since the last one left.

Test

1. It was a tragedy. Her husband did . . . . . . himself two years ago.
2. If I do any heavy work, I'm done in. (What does this mean?)
3. What has happened to your leg? (Give another expression with *do.*)
4. Since I started with arthritis, I've not been able to . . . . . . my clothes.
5. I could . . . . . . a hearing aid. I can't follow them on TV at all.

FIT

Fit someone/something in: *manage to find time to see someone or do something.* Doctor is booked up all morning but as it's urgent I'll try and fit you in.

Fit in with someone/something: *suit, harmonise with someone/something.* Do you think she will fit in with the rest of the team?

Fit someone/something out/up with: *equip.* These operating rooms are fitted out/up with the latest equipment.

Test

1. Can you fit Mrs Harper in? I know you are very busy. (What does *fit in* mean?)
2. The new research laboratory is equipped with the latest machinery. (Give an expression with *fit*).

GET

Get about: *(a) move from place to place.* I can't get about much now that I've got arthritis.
(b) spread (of news, rumour). It got about that people could be infected with AIDS from going to swimming baths.

Get something across: *communicate something to someone.* It's quite difficult to get across to my mother that she can't go on living alone.

Get along: *make progress.* Fine. You're getting along very well.

Get along with someone: *have a good relationship with somebody.* Do you get along with your family?

Get around (As Get about.)

Get at someone: *criticise someone repeatedly* (usually in continuous tenses). The other children are always getting at him and he's afraid of going to school now.

Get at someone/something: *reach.* Make sure you put these tablets somewhere where the children can't get at them.

Get away: *have a holiday.* You should try to get away for a few days after the operation.

Get something back: *recover something that was lost.* He's now got back the use of his arm which was paralysed by the stroke.

Get by: *manage, cope with life.* Single parent families often have a struggle to get by.

Get someone down: *depress.* All this quarrelling in the family gets me down.

Get something down: *swallow* (with difficulty). The tablets you gave me last time were so big I could hardly get them down.

Get into: *start bad habits.* How did she get into drugs?

Get (someone) off: *fall asleep, help someone to fall asleep.* It takes me ages to get the baby off at night.

Get off something: *leave work with permission.* He got a week off when his wife had a baby.

Get on: *(a) perform* (often used in questions with *how*). (i) How did you get on in the exam? (ii) I got on fine in medicine but I failed in English.
(b) progress. Take these tablets for a month and we'll see how you get on.

Get on with someone: *have a good relationship with.* He never got on with his boss.

Get out: *leave the house.* You must try to get out more. No wonder you are depressed, sitting here alone all day.

Get out of something: *give up a habit.* I wish I could get out of the habit of smoking after every meal.

Get over something: *(a) overcome.* No need to worry. I'm sure we can get over that problem.
(b) recover from disappointment, illness, shock. He's getting over the shock extremely well.

Get something over: *complete something difficult or unpleasant.* Thank goodness I've got the exams over.

Get something over to someone: *make someone understand.* You must get over to your husband the importance of remaining active as far as possible.

Get through something: *(a) consume, use a certain amount.* He gets through 40 cigarettes a day.
(b) pass an exam, test. Marvellous. I've got through my Final FRCS.

Get through to someone: *(a) make contact, communicate.* We are in despair. We just can't get through to our son at all.

(b) reach, especially by telephone. I've tried six times to speak to Dr Varley in Casualty but I can't get through.

Get together: *assemble, meet.* The Management and the Union should get together to settle this problem.

Get up: *(a) rise from bed.* Do you have to get up in the night to pass water?

(b) rise from seat. Please don't get up. Stay where you are.

Test

1. Does the pain in your legs stop you getting about? (What does this mean?)
2. Give two phrasal verbs with *get* that mean 'make progress'.
3. I must . . . . . . for a change. I've not had a holiday for years.
4. What kind of thing gets you down? (Give a suitable reply.)
5. My husband's always getting at the children. (What does this mean?)
6. Do you think I shall ever . . . . the use of my hand?
7. How do you cope without a job? (Give a phrasal verb for cope.)
8. Why did he get a week off? (Give a suitable reply.)
9. Come back in a month and we'll see how you've got on. (What does this mean?)
10. It's taken him a long time to . . . . . . the shock of losing his job.

GIVE

Give something back to someone: *restore, return.* The operation should give you back the use of your legs.

Give in (to someone/something): *stop arguing, fighting, trying, etc.* Mrs Spearey was marvellous. She had so much illness but she would not give in.

Give out: *(a) come to an end* (of food supplies, strength, etc.). I can't go on any longer. My strength has given out.

(b) fail, stop working. At the end of the 6-hour operation, the patient's heart gave out and he died.

Give something out: *distribute.* Those leaflets must be given out to all staff explaining the new safety regulations.

Give someone up: *(a) renounce hope.* The doctors had given her up months ago but she made a marvellous recovery.
(b) stop having a relationship with someone. Why don't you give him up if he treats you so badly?

Give something up: *stop doing something.* (i) It's going to be hard to give up smoking. (ii) I used to be a teacher but I gave it up last year.

Test

1. You've had bronchitis twice this year. You must . . . . . . smoking.
2. I've tried to understand his behaviour but now my patience has
. . . .
3. Doctors had no hope of her recovering. (Give a phrasal verb for this.)
4. Never . . . . Always keep trying.

GO

Go against something: *conflict with something.* Private medicine goes against the principles of the NHS set up in 1946.

Go ahead with something: *proceed with something.* The Government intends to go ahead with the reorganisation of the NHS.

Go along with someone/something: *(a) accompany.* Nurse, go along with Mrs Hooper to the X-Ray Department, will you?
(b) agree. I can't go along with your ideas for privatisation.

Go at someone: *attack physically or verbally.* The doctor went at her for neglecting her child.

Go back: *return.* I want you to go back to your GP with this letter.

Go by: *pass (of time)*. As time goes by, you'll get used to wearing the artificial limb.

Go by something: *form an opinion*. I know I look well but that's nothing to go by. I feel terrible.

Go down: *(a) be swallowed* (of food and drink). My food won't go down. (i.e. I have difficulty swallowing food.)
(b) be reduced in size, level, etc. How's your ankle? Well, the swelling has gone down but it's still very painful.
(c) become lower, fall (of prices, temperature, weight, etc.) (i) His temperature has gone down. (ii) I used to be 9st 7lbs and then I had an ulcer and went down to $8\frac{1}{2}$ stones.
(d) decrease in quality, deteriorate. Standards of behaviour have gone down in recent years.

Go down with something: *become ill with something*. All the children have gone down with measles.

Go for someone: *attack physically or verbally*. She went for him with a knife.

Go for someone/something: *Fetch*. Go for Sister, quickly.

Go in for: *(a) enter for an examination*. Hundreds of doctors go in for the FRCS every year.
(b) study for a particular profession. Are you going in for medicine like your father?

Go into something: *investigate*. The Paediatric Intensive Care Unit has been closed while the authorities go into the sudden deaths of ten babies.

Go off: *(a) deteriorate, get worse*. Her work has gone off since the accident.
(b) explode. She had to have plastic surgery after an oil heater went off in her face.
(c) faint, fall asleep, lose consciousness. (i) If he sees blood, he goes off. (ii) It takes me ages to go off. Sometimes I take a sleeping pill.
(d) go bad (of food or drink), *become unfit to eat or drink*. The food poisoning was caused by eating some meat that had gone off.

(e) stop (of pain). She's had this abdominal pain for a month and it won't go off.

Go off someone/something: *to lose one's liking or taste for someone/something.* (i) My wife's gone off me. (Usually means does not wish to continue sexual relationship.) (ii) I've gone off drink since my operation.

Go on: *continue.* (i) This trouble with your bowels has been going on for years, hasn't it? (When followed by a verb, it is in the . . .ing form.) (ii) Go on taking the tablets. (iii) Should I go on working while I'm pregnant, Doctor? It is often used negatively: (iv) I can't go on any longer like this. Can you give me something to help me, Doctor?

Go on something: *(a) begin to receive payments from the State because of unemployment.* We've had to go on social security as we've no other money coming in.
(b) go on the pill; begin to take the contraceptive pill. When did you first go on the pill?

Go on at someone: *to complain of someone's behaviour, work, etc.* He never stops going on at me.

Go out: *(a) be extinguished* (of fire, light, etc.). All the lights have gone out.
(b) leave the house. (i) I'm longing to go out again. (ii) You should be able to go out in a couple of days.

Go round: *spread from person to person* (of illness). There's a lot of flu going round at the moment.

Go round to: *pay a visit locally.* I went round to see my GP last week and he sent me here.

Go through: *experience, endure, suffer.* (i) When did he go through the phase of passing enormous stools? (ii) She's gone through a very bad patch recently (an unhappy or difficult time). (iii) I can't tell you what I've gone through since my husband died.

Go under: *(a) have an anaesthetic.* The patient went under at twelve and came round at four o'clock.

(b) die (slang). Do you think he's going to go under?

Go up: *rise* (of blood pressure, temperature, etc.). Your blood pressure has gone up again.

Go with someone: *accompany.* Have you anyone who can go with you to hospital?

Go without something: *manage without something.* (i) I have to go without food before I have the barium enema. (ii) They went without sleep for several days.

Test

1. Those tablets are so big. They won't go down. (What does this mean?)
2. What's happened to your weight in the last year? (Give a reply with an expression with *go.*)
3. When you stop drinking, does the pain . . . . . . ?
4. They went into the cause of death. (What does this mean?)
5. Last night I didn't . . . . . . until three in the morning. I feel so tired today.
6. What caused the food poisoning? (Give a suitable reply with an expression with *go.*)
7. Continue with the tablets till I see you again. (Replace 'continue' with a phrasal verb.)
8. When did you first go on the pill? (Explain what this means.)
9. There's a virus . . . . . . at the moment.
10. She . . . . . . a lot when she was nursing her husband.

KEEP

Keep away from someone/something: *avoid being near to.* Keep away from anyone with German measles if you are pregnant.

Keep someone/something back: *hold back.* (i) My disability will never keep me back. (ii) She couldn't keep back her tears.

Keep someone down: *dominate, oppress.* They had a difficult childhood. Their father kept them down.

Keep something down: *(a) keep something in the stomach* (often used negatively meaning to vomit). She's so thin because she can't keep anything down.

(b) not increase something (e.g. wages, prices, weight, etc.). (i) Keep your weight down. (ii) Restricting salt in the diet may help keep blood pressure down.

Keep someone from doing something: *prevent.* All this coughing keeps me from sleeping.

Keep off something: *not drink, eat, smoke, etc.* (i) Keep off fatty foods. (ii) You must keep off alcohol while you're taking these tablets.

Keep on doing something: *continue doing something, do something repeatedly.* The majority of women in the UK keep on working nowadays. (NB: keep doing something has the same meaning as keep on doing something.) Michael keeps getting stomach cramps.

Keep to something: *adhere to an agreement, a course, a diet, etc.* Keep to the diet for another two months and then we'll see how you are.

Keep someone up: *prevent someone from going to bed.* The baby kept us up all night with his crying.

Keep one's spirits, strength up: *not allow to fall.* (i) She is a very brave woman and always keeps her spirits up. (Remains cheerful.) (ii) You must eat to keep your strength up.

Keep up with someone/something: *move, progress at the same rate.* Elderly people find it difficult to keep up with all the changes of modern life.

Test

1. His father dominated them all when they were young. (Give an expression with *keep*.)
2. I feel dizzy and I can't keep anything down. (What does this mean?)

3. Did the doctor give you any instructions about your diet? (Give a suitable reply with *keep*.)
4. This disability . . . me . . . playing football.
5. He's been in hospital so long but he . . . . . . hoping he'll be home soon.
6. A busy doctor has not time to read all the latest medical books and journals. (Give an expression with *keep*.)

LET

Let someone down: *disappoint, fail to help.* Please come and see me when I'm in hospital. Don't let me down.

Let on to someone: *reveal a secret.* Don't let on to my parents I'm pregnant.

Let something out: *reveal a secret.* The press let it out that the hospital wards were closed because of cross-infection.

Let up: *(a) become less intense, severe.* If only this pain would let up for a while.
(b) relax one's efforts. After the train crash, the doctors worked night and day to treat the injured. Finally, they were able to let up a little.

Test

1. He's a good, reliable worker. He won't . . . you . . . . .
2. She doesn't want us to reveal to her boss that she's looking for another job. (Give an expression with *let* to replace 'to reveal'.)
3. They've worked 24 hours without stopping. (Replace 'stopping' by an expression with *let*.)

LOOK

Look after oneself/someone: *take care of.* (i) She is old and frail and needs to be properly looked after. (ii) Who will look after your children when you come into hospital?

Look after something: *be responsible for.* The laboratory technicians look after the equipment and keep it in good order.

Look at something: *examine carefully.* I want to look at your ear to see what's causing the trouble.

Look down on someone/something: *feel superior.* Her husband looks down on her because she hasn't been to university.

Look forward to doing something: *think of something in future with pleasure.* I'm looking forward to going home.

Look in: *make a short visit to someone's house.* Doctor will look in again this evening.

Look into something: *investigate.* We must look into this complaint. It says someone was left undressed one hour without being attended to.

Look on: *watch something without taking part.* Whilst the surgeon performed the delicate operation, doctors from many countries looked on.

Look on someone/something: *consider.* He's looked on as the most eminent surgeon in this field.

Look out: *be careful, watch out.* Look out! You'll burn yourself on that stove.

Look out for someone/something: *watch carefully for someone/something.* When examining patients, doctors look out for physical signs prevalent at particular ages.

Look over: *inspect buildings, papers, etc.* Can you look over this report before I submit it to the Working Party?

Look through something: *examine papers quickly.* Before handing in your exam papers, look through them for obvious mistakes.

Look to someone/something: *take care of.* The child-minder looks to the children while I'm at work.

Look up: *(a) improve.* How's Mrs Cox? Oh, she's looking up.
(b) raise eyes. Open your eyes now and look up. I'm going to put some drops in your eyes.

Look someone up: *visit someone, especially after a long time apart.* Do look me up when you next come to London.

Look something up: *search for a word, fact in a reference book.* If you don't understand the colloquial English your patient uses, look it up in the Manual.

Look up to someone: *admire, respect.* Most patients like to look up to their doctors.

Test

1. Look after yourself. (What does this mean?)
2. Will you examine my eye? I think I've got something in it. (Replace 'examine' by an expression with *look*.)
3. What do patients look forward to? (Give a few examples.)
4. There were six deaths in one week on the Surgical Ward. What did the authorities do?
5. You'll need permission to . . . . . . the new wing of the hospital.
6. Who looks to the children while you are at work? (Give a suitable reply.)
7. What do you do to find the required dose of a drug you are not familiar with?

MAKE

Make something of someone/something: *understand the nature or meaning of someone/something.* (i) We don't know what to make of this change in her behaviour. (ii) What do you make of it all?

Make off with something: *to steal something and run away with it.* The youth made off with the drugs he'd found.

Make someone out: *understand someone's behaviour.* We just can't make Mary out at all. She's very strange.

Make something out: *(a) manage to read.* Can you make out what this letter says?
(b) manage to understand. We'll have to get an interpreter. We just can't make out what this patient says.

(c) write a cheque, a prescription, etc. The doctor made out a prescription for my asthma.

Make up: *apply cosmetics.* Whenever I make up, I come out in a rash all over my face.

Make something up: *(a) invent a story, especially to deceive someone.* Stop making things up. What really happened?
(b) prepare a bed. Keep the patient here. The bed hasn't been made up yet.
(c) prepare medicine. Take this prescription to the pharmacist and he'll make it up for you.
(d) supply deficiency. It's not harmful to be a blood donor. The loss of blood is made up quite quickly in a healthy person.

Make up for something: *compensate.* No amount of money can make up for the loss of her husband.

Test

1. What do you do if you can't make out what your patient is saying? (Give a suitable reply.)
2. Does the rash start when you use cosmetics? (Replace use cosmetics by an expression with *make*.)
3. Could you please . . . . . . a bottle of medicine for my indigestion?
4. After three months in hospital, the boy will have to work very hard to make up for lost time. (What does this mean?)

PUT

Put something aside: *save money, etc., for future use.* Everything costs so much these days. I can't put anything aside for my old age.

Put someone away: *to confine someone to prison or mental hospital* (often used in passive). (i) The old man began to wander in the street at night so his family put him away. (ii) He was put away for 20 years for rape.

Put something away: *save money for future use.*

Put something back: *(a) drink large amount of alcohol* (slang). He must have put back a lot of beer to be in this state.
(b) impede. The accident has put back his hopes of climbing Everest.

Put something by: *save money for future use.* Have you anything put by?

Put something down: *(a) kill animal because it is old or sick.* I had to have my dog put down last week.
(b) place a baby in bed. I put him down at nine and he starts crying at eleven.
(c) write down. The doctor wants you to come again in two weeks. Put it down so you won't forget.

Put something down to: *consider something is caused by.* What do you put this rash down to, Doctor? I put it down to an allergy.

Put something forward: *propose, suggest.* The Junior Hospital Doctors Association put forward a proposal that they should not be on call for more than 70 hours at a stretch.

Put something in: *(a) install.* We aim to put a CT scanner in every hospital by next year.
(b) spend time on work. Junior doctors often put in over 12 hours' work a day.

Put in for something: *apply for a job.* He's put in for over 20 jobs without any success.

Put someone off (something): *(a) disturb, upset.* (i) He could never be a doctor. He's easily put off by the sight of blood. (ii) Food just puts me off at the moment.

Put someone off doing something: *dissuade someone from doing something.* We tried to put her off going into nursing but she'd made up her mind.

Put something off: *delay, postpone.* The operation has had to be put off owing to the strike.

Put something on: *(a) get dressed.* You can put your clothes on now, Mrs Turner.

(b) increase weight. Good. You've put on six pounds since we last saw you. (See page xv.)

Put someone out: *(a) anaesthetise.* They put me out and I came round three hours later (slang).

(b) annoy, upset. She was put out because they wouldn't let her go home.

Put something out: *(a) dislocate.* I'm afraid you've put your shoulder out.

(b) extinguish fire, light. Firemen soon put the fire out.

Put someone through: *connect on telephone.* Put me through to Casualty, will you?

Put someone up: *provide a bed and food.* I've nowhere to go. Can you put me up for a night?

Put something up: *(a) increase price.* My landlord has put the rent up by £10 a week so I'll have to go.

(b) raise. The pain's so bad I can't put my arms up to do my hair.

Put up with someone/something: *bear, tolerate.* (i) I'm afraid there's not much we can do about this condition. You'll have to put up with it. (ii) How did she put up with that violent husband for so long?

Test

1. Give three phrasal verbs with *put* to mean 'save for the future'.
2. Don't forget to . . . . . . your expenses when you go to the Conference.
3. What do you put the food poisoning down to? (Give a suitable answer.)
4. The nurse told the patient to dress. (Give an expression with *put.*)
5. Are you putting in for the Senior Registrar post? (What does this mean?)
6. I don't want to put you out. (What does this mean?)
7. Put me . . . to the Surgical Ward please.
8. What can't you put up with? Give some examples.

RUN

Run across someone/something: *to meet someone or find something by chance.* I've never run across this before. I think it's a case of botulism.

Run away from someone/something: *suddenly leave, escape.* He's always been a difficult child. He ran away from home at the age of six.

Run away with someone: *leave home, leave one's partner to start a relationship with someone else.* My husband has run away with a girl 20 years younger than himself.

Run someone/something down: *(a) hit and knock to the ground.* The cyclist was run down by a lorry.
(b) speak badly about someone. He's always running down his wife in public.

Run someone in: *arrest and take to police station.* He was run in for burglary with violence (slang).

Run into something: *(a) collide or crash into.* A man has just been brought into Casualty. He ran his car into a wall in the fog.
(b) get into danger, debt, trouble, etc. We've run into debt and my husband's drinking heavily.

Run something off: *make copies on a machine.* Could you run off 20 copies of this hand-out, please?

Run out of something: *come to an end* (of permits, supplies, time, etc.). (i) Make sure we've enough clean pyjamas this weekend. We mustn't run out. (ii) I'm nearly 80 you know. I'm running out of time. (iii) My energy is running out.

Run over someone: (of a vehicle) *knock someone down and pass over body.* He's been run over and has broken his ribs.

Run over something: *read quickly, repeat.* Will you just run over the facts again?

Run through something: *(a) discuss, examine, read quickly.* I've run through the names of patients admitted this week but your son's is not there.

(b) spend carelessly, wastefully They have run through thousands of pounds on advertising.

(c) use up. We run through a lot of disposable gloves in the gynaecological clinic.

Run up something: *accumulate bills.* Why did you run up such large bills?

Test

1. Her husband had a stroke after he . . . . . . debt.
2. I need 100 copies of this report. Could you . . . them . . . by 2 o'clock?
3. The stock of disposable syringes has come to an end. (Replace by an expression with *run*.)
4. I must run through my exam paper before I give it in. (What does 'run through' mean?)
5. Make sure we've enough oxygen. We mustn't . . . .

SEND

Send for someone: *tell someone to come.* He's failing. Send for the ambulance.

Send for something: *order something to be delivered.* Send for 200 disposable syringes, will you?

Send off something: *post.* Don't forget to send off those letters today.

Send out something: *emit.* Factories and houses used to send out clouds of black smoke before the Clean Air Act was passed.

Test

1. I smell burning . . . . . . the fire brigade.
2. Order a copy of this for all new staff, will you? (Replace 'order' with an expression with *send*.)

3. Factories aren't allowed to emit black smoke nowadays. (What does 'emit' mean?)

SET

Set aside something: *(a) save money for particular purpose.* She sets aside a bit of money every month for a holiday.
(b) keep time for a particular purpose. You must set aside half an hour a day to practise the relaxation exercises.

Set back someone/something: *delay progress of someone/something.* (i) Mr Deakin was making a good recovery after his operation but unfortunately a complication has set him back. (ii) Work on the new theatre has been set back three months.

Set in: *begin and seem likely to continue* (of rain, winter, infection, etc.). (i) When cold weather sets in, the elderly must take precautions to care for themselves. (ii) You can see gangrene has set in to your left leg and we have no alternative but to remove it.

Set on someone: *attack.* I got this bite when a dog set on me.

Set someone up: *make better, healthier.* A week by the sea will set you up after the hysterectomy.

Set up something: *begin to make a noise, row.* John set up screaming and went on for hours.

Test

1. I know you are busy but you must . . . . . . a particular time to do your exercises.
2. Developing pneumonia after the operation has delayed his progress. (Give an expression with *set* to replace 'delayed his progress'.)
3. Why did they amputate his left leg? (Give an answer using *set*.)
4. A good holiday will set you up. (What does this mean?)

TAKE

Take after someone: *resemble in appearance or character.* I'm worried about Jane. She's so different from me. She takes after her father.

Take something away: *(a) cause a feeling, etc. to disappear.* (i) I'll give you some tablets to take the pain away. (ii) All this worry has taken my appetite away.
(b) remove. They've taken her womb away.

Take someone away from someone/something: *remove.* When sexual abuse was suspected, the children were taken away from their parents on the recommendation of social workers.

Take something down: *record, write something.* Can you take down the history?

Take something in: *absorb, understand by listening or reading.* Patients often find it difficult to take in what the doctor tells them.

Take something off: *(a) amputate part of body.* His left arm had to be taken off below the elbow.
(b) have time away from work for special purpose. I'm taking next week off to be at home when my wife comes out of hospital.
(c) lose weight by dieting. You're overweight. I want you to take off a stone. Go and see the dietitian. (See page 000.)
(d) remove part of clothing. You needn't take off all your clothes. Just your shirt and trousers.

Take on something: *agree to do work, have responsibility.* Don't take on too much for the next six weeks.

Take something out: *remove or extract.* (i) I must have this tooth taken out. It's giving me a lot of pain. (ii) She's going into hospital to have her appendix taken out. (iii) We're going to take the stitches out tomorrow.

Take something over from someone: *take control, responsibility from someone else.* Can you take over my bleep for ten minutes while I make a 'phone call overseas?

Take to someone: *develop a liking for someone.* I never took to my daughter-in-law. She's caused so much trouble in the family.

Take to something/doing something: *begin to do something as a habit.* (i) We need help. Our only son has taken to drugs. (ii) He's taken to going for long walks late at night.

Take up something: *(a) absorb, occupy time.* Medicine takes up all his time and energy.
(b) start a job. We expect you to take up your duties on 1st January.
(c) start a profession, hobby, etc. He's thinking of taking up psychiatry as a career.

Test

1. Did they take my ovaries away? (What does this mean?)
2. Don't forget to . . . . . . the details of her reaction to the new treatment.
3. It's too much. I simply can't absorb all the information you've given me. (Replace 'absorb' by an expression with *take*.)
4. I wish I could . . . . . . some weight. Can you help me?
5. You've just had a coronary. Rest for six weeks and don't . . . . . . too much after that.
6. The dentist extracted two teeth. (Give an expression with *take*.)
7. When do you take up your new job? (Give a suitable reply.)

TURN

Turn against someone: *become hostile to.* After our divorce, my wife tried to turn the children against me.

Turn someone away: *refuse to give help.* Doctors cannot turn sick people away.

Turn someone/something down: *(a) reject an idea, person, proposal.* They turned me down as a pilot because of my eyesight. *(b) reduce volume of gas, sound, etc.* When they turn down the television I can't hear a thing.

Turn in: *(a) go to bed* (slang). It's usually two o'clock before I turn in.
(b) be pigeon-toed. He walks with his toes turned in.

Turn something in: *stop doing something* (slang). The job was ruining my health so although I loved it, I had to turn it in.

Turn someone off: *cause someone to be disgusted by something or not sexually attracted to someone.* His drinking and bad breath turned me off.

Turn something off *(a) stop the flow of electricity, gas, etc.* Don't forget to turn off the machine before you leave the building.
(b) stop radio, TV. The TV is going all day. He never turns it off.

Turn on someone: *attack.* As I left the building, the guard dog turned on me and bit my leg.

Turn someone on: *give great pleasure, excite sexually.* Psychedelic drugs turn you on very quickly.

Turn something on: *allow gas, electricity, water to flow.* Make sure the computer on which the records are stored is turned on first thing.

Turn something out: *extinguish light or fire.* Please turn out the lights before going home.

Turn someone out: *force someone to leave a place.* I've nowhere to sleep. My landlord has turned me out.

Turn over: *change position of body by rolling.* Turn over onto your left side and draw your knees to your chest.

Turn someone/something round: *face in different direction.* Turn round and let me look at your back.

Turn to someone/something: *go for advice, help.* (i) Hospitals are good places to turn to when you are ill. (ii) Sadly, when his wife left him he turned to drink for solace.

Turn up: *(a) appear, arrive.* Mr Fox hasn't turned up yet for his appointment.
(b) be found, by chance, after being lost. Thank goodness those keys have turned up. We thought they'd been stolen.

Turn something up: *increase volume of radio, TV, etc.* I have to turn up my hearing aid to listen to the news.

Test

1. I can't . . . you . . . when you are in this state. (Give two possible expressions with *turn* and explain their meaning.)
2. What turned her off her husband? (Give a suitable reply.)
3. You forgot to . . . . . . the lights when you left yesterday.
4. Now I want you to roll over onto your right side. (Give an expression with *turn*.)
5. I've no money, no home and nobody to . . . .
6. Half the patients haven't turned up to the Clinic today. (What does this mean?)

ANSWERS TO TESTS ON PHRASAL VERBS

Break

1. Because she heard she had to have her leg amputated.
2. It has broken down.
3. Because cholera has broken out.
4. I break out in a rash.
5. The strain of nursing his wife.

Bring

1. Heavy drinking.
2. bring on
3. lower, reduce
4. Try to bring him round/to.
5. My grandmother.

Come

1. across
2. come along and come on
3. Returning to memory.
4. down
5. To present oneself with help, information.
6. So we can do some tests. So we can keep her under observation.
7. It first came on a week ago.
8. regained consciousness

Cut

1. Yes. He told me to cut down (on) the fats/the cigarettes.
2. off
3. cut off
4. Stop eating.
5. He felt cut up. (Upset emotionally.)

Do

1. away with
2. Exhausted.
3. What have you done to your leg?
4. do up
5. do with

Fit

1. Manage to find time to see her.
2. fitted out/up with

Get

1. Moving from place to place.
2. get along and get on
3. get away
4. Failing an exam, being without a job, being far from home and family.
5. Criticise repeatedly.
6. get back
7. get by
8. Because his wife had a baby, the children were ill, his mother died, etc.
9. We'll see how you have progressed, if you are any better.
10. get over

Give

1. give up
2. given out
3. Doctors had given her up.
4. give in

Go

1. They are difficult to swallow.
2. It's gone down to $8\frac{1}{2}$ stone.
3. go off
4. Investigated.
5. go off
6. Eating some meat that had gone off.
7. go on
8. Start taking the contraceptive pill.
9. going round
10. went through

Keep

1. His father kept them down when they were young.
2. I have vertigo and I have vomited.
3. Yes, he told me to keep off fatty foods and alcohol. He told me to keep to the diet for another two months.
4. keeps me from
5. keeps on
6. A busy doctor can't keep up with his subject.

Let

1. let you down
2. let on
3. letting up

Look

1. Take care of yourself.
2. look at
3. They look forward to having visitors, feeling better and going home.
4. They looked into the matter.
5. look over

6. My mother, a friend, a child-minder.
7. Look it up in the British National Formulary.

Make

1. Ask the patient to repeat it, to speak slower, louder. If the patient's English is inadequate, get an interpreter to help.
2. make up
3. make up
4. to compensate

Put

1. put aside, put away and put by
2. put down
3. I put it down to some shell fish I ate.
4. to put her clothes on
5. Are you applying for the post?
6. annoy, upset
7. through
8. Severe pain, extreme noise, cold weather, etc.

Run

1. ran into
2. run off
3. run out
4. check, read quickly
5. run out

Send

1. Send for
2. Send for
3. send out

Set

1. set aside
2. set him back
3. Because gangrene had set in.
4. make you feel better

Take

1. remove
2. take down
3. take in
4. take off
5. take on
6. took out
7. Next month. In Janaury.

Turn

1. Turn you away means refuse to help you.
   Turn you out means force you to leave.
2. His drinking, his violence.
3. turn off, turn out
4. turn over
5. turn to
6. appeared at, come to

10 Idioms

PARTS OF THE BODY

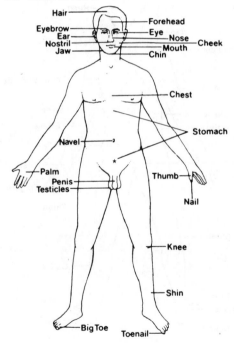

Fig. 1

* As used colloquially by patient and often referred to as *tummy*.

241

IDIOMS

The English language has thousands of idioms. By an idiom we mean a number of words which, when taken together, have a different meaning from that of each separate word.

The reason for including these idioms of parts of the body is that although you may never need to *use* them yourself, you should be able to *recognise* them. You may be told by a patient that by the end of the day he is 'on his knees' and you must realise that he is using the word 'knee' idiomatically. What he means is that he is extremely tired after work and feels like collapsing.

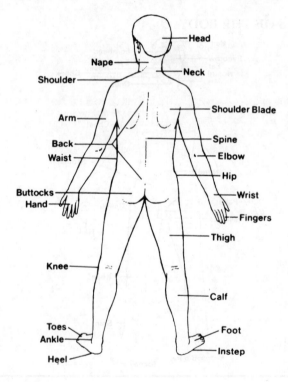

Fig. 2

A women may tell you of her worries and say she has just managed to 'keep her head above water'. If you are not familiar with the idiom, you may think she has tried to save herself from drowning but, in fact, she means that she is terribly short of money and is having a struggle to keep out of debt.

Words and phrases connected with parts of the body have also been included, such as, chesty, throaty and to speak through one's nose. It is essential that you understand these.

It should be noticed that under 'Nail' appear several idioms which refer to other meanings of the word than the nail of the body. They have been included because they are all commonly used and you should be familiar with them.

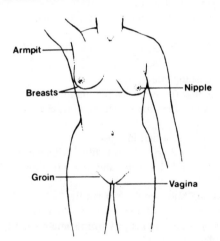

Fig. 3

Arm

A shot in the arm: something that does a person good.

To give one's right arm (usually with *would*): to be willing to make a sacrifice to get something.

To keep someone at arm's length: to avoid being friendly.

To stand by with folded arms: to do nothing when action seems necessary.

To welcome someone with open arms: to greet warmly.

Back

To back a horse: to place money on a horse in a race, to bet.
To back down: to be less demanding than before.
To back out: to withdraw from.
To back someone or something: to give one's support.
To be on one's back: to be ill in bed.
To break one's back: to overwork.
To do something behind someone's back: to act deceitfully.
To have one's back to the wall: to be struggling against great difficulties.
To put, (get, set) someone's back up: to make someone angry.
To see the back of someone/something: to get rid of someone/something that is annoying, unpleasant.
To turn one's back on: to abandon, to refuse to help.

Blood

A young blood: dashing young man.
Bad blood: ill feeling, (between people, nations).
Blood is thicker than water: one's own relations come before all other people.
His blood is up: he is in a fighting mood.
His blood ran cold in his veins: he was filled with terror.
It is more than flesh and blood can stand: too much for human beings to endure.
One's own flesh and blood: one's own family.
To do something in cold blood: deliberately; when one is not angry.
To get blood out of a stone: to get pity from someone hard; to achieve the impossible.
To get someone's blood up: to provoke someone very much.
To have fresh, new blood: to have new members in a business, family or society.
To make one's blood boil: to make one very angry.
To run in the blood: to have an inherited quality.

Bone

A bone of contention: the subject of constant disagreement.

He will never make old bones: will not live to an old age.

To be all skin and bones: very thin.

To be bone dry: completely dry.

To be bone-idle: completely idle.

To feel something in one's bones: to feel quite sure about something without proof.

To have a bone to pick with someone: to wish to complain about something.

To make no bones about doing something: to have no hesitation in doing something. (Usually unpleasant.)

Brain

A brain-child: original idea of a person or group.

A brain-drain: movement of trained and qualified workers to other countries (usually for better conditions).

A brain-storm: cerebral disturbance; a mental aberration (informal).

A brain-storming session: a method of solving problems in which many people suggest ideas which are then discussed.

A brain-wave: a sudden inspiration or clever idea.

A scatter-brained person: a careless, forgetful person.

Brain-fag: mental exhaustion.

Brain fever: encephalitis.

Brain-washing: forcing someone to change his beliefs by use of extreme mental pressure.

Brainy: clever.

To blow one's brain out: to shoot oneself in the head.

To have something on the brain: to be obsessive about something.

To pick someone's brains: to find out someone's good ideas and use them.

To rack one's brains: to think very hard; to solve a problem or remember something.

Breast

To make a clean breast of something: to confess everything.

Brow (forehead), Brows (arch of hair above eyes)

A high-brow: someone interested in intellectual matters and culture.

A low-brow: someone showing little interest in intellectual matters and culture.

To browbeat someone into doing something: to intimidate someone with severe looks and words, bully.

To knit one's brows: to frown.

Cheek

Cheek: impudence, disrespectful speech.

Cheeks: buttocks.

To be cheeky: to be impudent, disrespectful.

To cheek someone: to speak impudently to someone.

To have the cheek to do something: to be bold, rude enough to do something.

Chest

To be chesty: to have trouble with one's lungs.

To cock one's chest: to boast about oneself.

To get something off one's chest: to free one's mind by speaking about something that was troubling one.

Get that across your chest! Eat that! (Usually a large, nourishing meal.)

To puff one's chest out: to be proud of oneself.

Chin

A chin: a talk.

Chin up: be brave.

To be up to the chin in work, etc.: to have too much work to do.

To chin: to talk, gossip.

To have a chin-wag: to talk with friends about unimportant matters; to chatter.

To keep one's chin up: to be brave, to be cheerful in the face of difficulties.

Ears

To be all ears: to listen very carefully.

To box someone's ears: to smack someone on the ears.

To come to one's ears: to hear a rumour.

To earmark: to put someone/something aside for a special purpose.

To fall on deaf ears: to pass unnoticed.

To give one's ears for something: to be prepared to do anything to get what one desires.

In at one ear and out at the other: ignored or quickly forgotten advice.

To have a person's ear: to have the favourable attention of someone.

To have a word in someone's ear: to speak in private.

To keep one's ear to the ground: to listen carefully.

To play it by ear: to do what seems best at the time.

To prick up one's ears: to have one's attention suddenly aroused.

To send someone away with a flea in his ear: to criticise someone severely so that he goes away unhappily.

To set people by the ears: to cause them to quarrel.

To turn a deaf ear: to ignore, pretend not to hear.

Elbow

Elbow-grease: vigorous polishing; hard work.

Elbow-room: plenty of room to move freely.

Out-at-elbows: of a coat, worn out; of a person, poor.

To elbow one's way through a crowd: to push with one's elbows.

To raise the elbow: to drink too much.

Eye

A blue-eyed boy: a pet, favourite.

A sight for sore eyes: someone or something very welcome, pleasant.

A sore eye: an inflamed eye.

An eye for an eye: to punish those who hurt us.

An eye-opener: an event or piece of news which causes surprise.

An eyesore: a very unpleasant thing to look at.

Eyeball to eyeball: face to face with someone.

Eye-wash: lotion for bathing eyes; words or actions intended to mislead.

Green-eyed: jealous.

In the eyes of: in the opinion of.

In the mind's eye: imagining in the mind.

In the public eye: to be watched by the public constantly.

The apple of one's eye: someone or something very precious.

To be up to the eyes in work: to have far too much work to do.

To catch someone's eye: to attract someone's attention.

To cry one's eyes out: to weep very much.

To do something with one's eyes open: to act knowing the results of the action.

To eye someone: to look at carefully, admiringly, jealously, etc.

To get (or give) a black eye: to receive (or give) a blow on the eye so that the skin around it goes black.

To give someone the glad eye: to encourage someone to be amorous.

To have an eye for: to have a liking or ability to do something; to have good judgement on something.

To have an eye on/to the main chance: to think and work with one's own advantage always in view.

To have half an eye on: to give little attention to something.

To have one's eyes opened: to be forced to see reality.

To keep an eye on someone/something: to watch carefully.

To keep one's eye open for: to watch carefully.

To keep one's eyes skinned: to be very watchful.

To make eyes at someone: to look at someone (usually of the opposite sex) with open admiration and invitation.

To pull the wool over someone's eyes: to try to hide the truth from someone.

To run one's eye over: to look quickly at, to glance at.

To see eye to eye with someone: to have the same ideas; to agree.

To turn a blind eye: to ignore deliberately, pretend not to see.

Face

Face-ache: neuralgia.

Let's face it: let's be honest with each other.

To be a slap in the face: a sudden disappointment, rejection.

To face the music: to face criticism/punishment as a result of one's own actions.

To face up to something: to meet courageously (usually difficulties).

To fly in the face of convention, rules, etc.: to defy, disobey openly.

To have a face as long as a fiddle: to look depressed.

To keep a straight face: not laugh. (Often used negatively — e.g. 'I couldn't keep a straight face').

To look someone in the face: to look directly at someone.

To lose face: to be humiliated, to be put to shame.

To make/pull a face: to grimace.

To pull a long face: to look displeased, disappointed, depressed.

To put a brave/good face on it: to behave as if circumstances are better than they really are.

To save one's face: to try to avoid shaming oneself openly.

To set one's face against: to oppose.

To show one's face: to appear, be seen.

To stare one in the face: something that is obvious, clear to see.

Feet (see Foot)

Fingers

Not to raise (lift, stir) a finger to help someone: to refuse to be of any help.

One's fingers itch to do something: one wishes very much to do something.

To be all fingers and thumbs: to be clumsy with one's hands often due to nervousness.

To be light-fingered: to steal easily.

To burn one's fingers: to get into trouble by interfering in other people's affairs.

To finger: to touch.

To get/pull one's finger out: to stop being lazy, work harder (informal).

To have a finger in every pie: to be involved in many activities.

To have butter-fingers: to let things slip out of the hands.

To have something at one's finger-tips: to know perfectly.

To keep one's fingers crossed (for someone): hope for luck with a problem or difficulty.

To lay/put one's finger on something: to realise the most important aspect of a matter.

To let something slip through one's fingers: to lose hold of, allow to escape (usually of opportunities).

To twist a person round one's finger: to have someone in one's power so that they do all one wishes.

To work one's fingers to the bone: to work very hard.

Flesh

Flesh wound: one not reaching bone or a vital organ.

One's own flesh and blood: one's own family.

Proud flesh: new flesh coming from a wound.

Sins of the flesh: sexual sins.

To be neither fish nor flesh: to be of indefinite character.

To have one's pound of flesh: to insist cruelly on repayment.

To lose flesh: to get thinner.

To make one's flesh creep: to be terrified so that one's skin seems to move.

To put on flesh: to get fatter.

To see someone in the flesh: actually to see someone.

Foot, Feet

My foot!: Nonsense! Rubbish!

Not to let the grass grow under one's feet: to act quickly when one has made a decision.

To be on one's feet: to be in reasonable health; to be standing.

To be run off one's feet: to be so busy one cannot sit down.

To dog one's footsteps: to follow one constantly and so cause irritation.

To drag one's feet: to be slow to take action.

To fall on one's feet: to be lucky.

To fall over one's feet to be kind, helpful, etc.: to make a great effort.

To find one's feet: to be comfortably settled in a new job, situation, etc.

To foot the bill: to pay.

To get cold feet: to be afraid, discouraged.

To go on foot: to walk.

To have one foot in the grave: to be very ill, close to death.

To have one's feet on the ground: to be practical, sensible.

To have the world at one's feet: to be very successful.

To put one's best foot forward: to walk quickly, to work quickly.

To put one's feet up: to relax, rest.

To put one's foot down: to be firm, protest.

To put one's foot in it: to do or say something that causes anger, trouble.

To set someone on his feet: to help, usually with money, to start a business, etc.

To stand on one's own feet: to be independent.

To step off on the wrong foot: to start something in the wrong way.

Hair

A hair's breadth: a very small distance.

Hair-raising (stories): terrifying.

Not turn a hair: to show no sign of fear or emotional upset.

To a hair: exactly (usually of weight).

To have one's hair standing on end: to be terrified.

To have someone by the short hairs: to have control over them.

To keep one's hair on: not to grow angry.

To let down one's hair: to act freely, to be uninhibited.

To split hairs: to argue about very small, unimportant differences.

Hand

A right-hand man: someone who can be relied on for help and advice.

At first hand: directly.

Hands off! Do not touch.

Never to do a hand's turn: never make the slightest effort.

To be a handful: to be difficult to control.

To be an old hand at something: to be experienced.

To be hand-in-glove with someone: to be extremely friendly (usually planning something together).

To be high-handed: to be arrogant.

To be off-hand: to be abrupt in manner, casual.

To be off one's hands: to be no longer responsible for someone or something.

To be open-handed: to be generous with money.

To be out of hand (of children, a situation, etc.): to be out of control.

To be under-hand: to be deceitful, dishonest, not open.

To eat out of someone's hand: to do whatever one wishes.

To force someone's hand: to make someone do something.

To get one's hand in: to get to know how to do something.

To give/lend someone a hand: to help someone physically.

To give someone a free hand: to allow someone to do as he wishes.

To hand: to give, to offer.

To have a hand in something: to share in the activity.

To have one's hands full: to be extremely busy.

To have one's hands tied: to be unable to act in the way one wishes.

To have the upper hand over someone: to dominate.

To have time on one's hands: to have plenty of free time.

To keep one's hand in: to be in practice.

To lay hands on: to seize, touch (often used negatively).

To live from hand to mouth: to live from day to day; without regular money.

To play into someone's hands: to do something which helps one's opponent.

To rule with a heavy hand: to rule severely.

To say off-hand: to give an answer immediately from memory.

To take one's courage in both hands: to force oneself to do something difficult, unpleasant.

To take someone in hand: to try to improve someone's behaviour.

To try one's hand at something: to make an attempt to do something new.

To wait on someone hand and foot: to attend to someone's needs with great care.

To wash one's hands of someone/something: to have nothing more to do with.

Head

A headache: a pain in the head; a difficult problem.

From head to foot/toe: completely; all over the person.

It is on his head: he is responsible for it.

Not to know whether one is standing on one's head or one's heels: to be in a state of extreme confusion.

To be big-headed: to be conceited.

To be block-headed: to be dull, stupid.

To be fat-headed: to be stupid.

To be hard-headed: to be practical, unsentimental.

To be head and shoulders above others: to be much taller; to be far superior.

To be head over heels in love: completely, very much.

To be hot-headed: to be hasty, impulsive.

To be above/over one's head: too difficult to understand.

To be pig-headed: to be obstinate.

To be soft-headed: to be simple-minded.

To be touched in the head: to be slightly mad.

To bite a person's head off: to speak sharply, angrily to someone.

To bury one's head in the sand: to avoid facing facts by pretending not to see them.

To come to a head: to reach a crisis.

To do something on one's head: to do something extremely easily.

To eat one's head off: to eat an excessive amount.

To get something into one's head: be convinced that something is true.

To go off one's head: to become crazy, mad.

To go to one's head: to make one excited, to intoxicate one.

To have a good head for business: to have a natural aptitude for it.

To have a good head-piece: to have plenty of brains.

To have a head: to have a headache, often from drinking too much.

To have a head like a sieve: to be very forgetful.

To have an old head on young shoulders: to be wise beyond one's years.

To have one's head screwed on the right way: to be intelligent, full of common sense, especially in practical matters.

To have something hanging over one's head: to have some danger, something unpleasant going to happen soon.

To head off: to divert a person from someone or something.

To heap coals of fire on a person's head: to treat a person well who has treated oneself badly.

To hit the nail on the head: to guess right, to reach the correct conclusion.

To keep one's head: to stay calm in a difficult situation.

To keep one's head above water: to keep out of debt.

To knock on the head: to destroy, disrupt an idea, plan, etc.

To let someone have his head: to let him do as he wishes.

To lose one's head: to lose one's self-control in a difficult situation.

To make head, headway: to make progress.

To make head or tail of something: to understand it. (Usually used negatively: 'I couldn't make head or tail of the letter he sent me'.)

To put something out of one's head: to forget it deliberately, to stop thinking about it.

To put things into someone's head: to suggest things to him.

To run/knock one's head against a stone wall: to do something that will fail, because of opposition.

To talk someone's head off: to talk so much that the other person is weary.

To take it into one's head: to make a sudden decision.

Two heads are better than one: two people know more together than one person.

Heart

After one's own heart: a person sharing one's own interests, opinions.

At heart: basically, deep down.

Have a heart! Be reasonable; don't be unkind!

Heartache: deep sorrow.

Heartburn: pain in chest as a result of indigestion.

Heart-felt sympathy: deepest sympathy.

Heart-searching: doubts, uncertainties.

In one's heart of hearts: deep down in oneself.

Not to have the heart to do something: not to have the courage to do something.

The heart of the matter: the essence, the vital part.

To be down-hearted: to be depressed.

To be good at heart: to be good basically.

To be half-hearted about something: not to be very enthusiastic.

To be hard-hearted: to be hard, unkind.

To be heartless: to be unkind, unsympathetic.

To be hearty: to be cheerful.

To be in good heart: to be cheerful, confident.

To be lion-hearted: to be very brave.

To be soft-hearted: to be kind, sympathetic.

To be stout-hearted: to be very brave.

To break one's heart: to be overwhelmed with sorrow.

To cause heartache: to cause suffering.

To cry one's heart out: to cry excessively.

To eat one's heart out: to fret, worry excessively.

To have a big heart: to be warm, generous.

To have a heart-to-heart talk with someone: to speak openly, hiding nothing.

To have a hearty appetite: to have a very good appetite.

To have no heart: to be hard, insensitive.

To have no heart for something: to have no enthusiasm for something.

To have one's heart in one's boots: to be depressed, to feel hopeless.

To have one's heart in one's mouth: to be very afraid.

To know, learn, say by heart: to know word for word by memory.

To lose heart: to have no hope, to become discouraged, (often used negatively): 'Don't lose heart: keep on hoping'.

To lose one's heart: to fall in love.

To put one's heart into something: to do something with enthusiasm.

To set one's heart on something: to want something very much.

To take heart: to become more hopeful.

To take someone to one's heart: to feel deep affection for someone.

To take something to heart: to be upset; to worry too much about things.

To tear one's heart-strings: to hurt one very deeply.

Whole-hearted: complete, without doubts.

Heel(s)

A heel: a completely unreliable person.

An/one's Achilles heel: weak or vulnerable point, especially of character.

Not to know whether one is standing on one's head or one's heels: to be in a state of extreme confusion.

To be down at heel: poorly dressed and in a state of poverty.

To be head over heels in love: completely, very much.

To bring someone to heel: to put under control.

To carry with the heels first: as a dead body.

To come on the heels of: to follow immediately.

To kick one's heels: to stand waiting idly, impatiently.

To leave to cool his heels: to make someone wait deliberately.

To show a clean pair of heels: to run away.

To take to one's heels: to run away.

Knee

To be knee-deep in something: deeply involved in.

To be on one's knees: to kneel, especially when praying; to be completely exhausted.

To bring someone to his knees: to make him submit, stop fighting.

To go down on one's knees to someone: to beg for something.

Knuckles

To knuckle down to a job: to work as hard as one can.

To knuckle under: to accept defeat.

To rap someone's knuckles: to reprimand.

Lap (waist to knees of one sitting)

In the lap of the gods: uncertain future.

In the lap of luxury: in great comfort and luxury.

Leg

A blackleg: a person who continues working when others are on strike.

Not to have a leg to stand on: have no good reason to support one's argument.

The boot is on the other leg: the truth is the opposite of what one believes.

To be all legs: to be overgrown.

To be on one's last legs: to be close to death; utterly weary.

To find one's legs: to be able to stand and walk (usually after an illness).

To get one's sea-legs: to become used to the movement of a ship.

To give someone a leg up: to help someone.

To pull someone's leg: to tease someone.

To show a leg: to get out of bed.

To stretch one's legs: to go for a walk.

To walk someone off his legs: to tire him out with walking.

Lip

Lip: saucy talk, impudence.

None of your lip!: Don't speak to me like that.

Lip-language, reading, speaking: use of the movement of the lips to and by the deaf and dumb.

A word escapes one's lips: something is said without thought.

To bite one's lip: to stop oneself from saying something; to hide emotion.

To curl one's lip: to show scorn.

To hang on someone's lip: to listen with great care.

To have sealed lips: to be silent about something.

To keep a stiff upper lip: to bear troubles without showing emotion.

To lick one's lips: to show appreciation of food (or sometimes other things).

To pay lip service to principles, etc.: to say one believes in something but not to act accordingly.

Mind

Mind: memory, remembrance.

Mind-blowing: (of drugs, etc.) causing ecstasy, excitement.

Mind-boggling: astonishing, extraordinary.

Never mind: It doesn't matter; don't worry.

To be not in one's right mind: to be mad.

To be out of one's mind: to be mad.

To bear something in mind: to remember.

To bend someone's mind: to influence the mind so that it is permanently affected.

To give someone a piece of one's mind: to speak openly and critically.

To go out of one's mind: to go mad: 'He went out of his mind in the end.'; to be forgotten: 'I'm so sorry. It went out of my mind.'

To have a good mind to do something: to have almost decided to do something.

To have presence of mind: to act and think quickly in emergencies.

To have something on one's mind: to be worried about something.

To know one's own mind: to be definite about what one wants.

To make up one's mind: to decide.

To mind: (a) to be careful (used very often in orders): 'Mind the step: be careful of the step.' 'Mind the car: get out of the way of the car.' (b) to care (often used negatively): 'I don't mind what she does or says.' (c) to object (used mainly interrogatively and negatively): 'I don't mind going to hospital to have my baby.' Note the polite request: Would you mind + -ing form of the verb: 'Would you mind lying on the couch?'

(d) to take care of: 'She had no-one to mind the baby when she went to work.' Noun: a baby-minder.

To mind one's own business: not to interfere in the affairs of other people.

To mind one's p's and q's: to be careful what one says and does.

To take a load/weight off someone's mind: cause great relief.

Mouth

Mouth: impudent talk, rudeness.

To be down in the mouth: to be depressed.

To look as if butter would not melt in one's mouth: to look innocent, incapable of badness.

To make one's mouth water: to cause saliva to flow at the sight of food.

To put words into someone's mouth: to tell someone what to say.

To take the words out of someone's mouth: to say what someone was about to say.

Nail(s)

To be as hard as nails: to be very hard; merciless.

To be as right as nails to be perfectly fit.

To fight tooth and nail: to fight fiercely, vigorously.

To hit the nail on the head: to say the right thing; guess right.

To nail someone down: to make someone give a definite statement; details.

To pay on the nail: to pay at once.

To put a nail in one's coffin: to do something that will shorten one's life.

Neck

Neck: boldness, impertinence, disrespect.

Neck or nothing: desperately risking everything for success.

Stiff-necked: obstinate, proud, stubborn.

To be a pain in the neck: to be a nuisance and pest to someone.

To be up to the neck in debt, work: to be completely immersed in.

To break one's neck to do something: work extremely hard to do something.

To get it in the neck: to be severely punished.

To have the neck to do something: to be rude enough to do something.

To neck: to hug and kiss someone intimately.

To run neck and neck: to be level with someone in a competition.

To save one's neck: to save oneself from punishment.

To stick one's neck out: to act or speak in a way which exposes one to harm or criticism.

To talk out of the back of one's neck: to talk nonsense.

To throw someone out neck and crop: to throw someone out head first, bodily.

Nerve

Not to know what nerves are: to have a calm temperament.

To be a bundle of nerves: in a very nervous state.

To get on one's nerves: to annoy or irritate very much.

To have a fit of nerves: to be in a nervous state.

To have iron/steel nerves: not to be easily upset or frightened.

To have the nerve to do something: to be brave, to be impudent enough.

To lose one's nerves: to become frightened and unsure of oneself.

To nerve oneself to do something: to use all one's strength, mental and physical.

To strain every nerve: to make a great effort.

What a nerve!: What impudence!

Nose

A nosey parker: a person who tries to find out about other people's private affairs.

To cut off one's nose to spite one's face: to do something in anger to hurt someone else which also hurts oneself.

To follow one's nose: to go straight on; to act on instinct.

To have a good nose: to have a good sense of smell.

To keep one's nose to the grindstone: to work hard over a long period.

To lead someone by the nose: to make someone do anything one wishes.

To look down one's nose at someone: to regard someone as inferior.

To nose about: to look enquiringly everywhere.

To pay through the nose: to pay an excessive price.

To poke one's nose into something: to try to find out about people and things which do not concern one.

To put someone's nose out of joint: to do something to irritate or upset someone.

To see no further than one's nose: not to be able to imagine the future or any situation other than the current one.

To speak through one's nose: to speak with a nasal sound (often as a result of adenoids).

To turn up one's nose: to show dislike or disapproval.

Palm

To grease someone's palm: to bribe him, offer money for information, etc.

To palm something off on someone: to sell something that is worthless or damaged.

Shoulder

A shoulder to cry on: someone who listens to one's problems with sympathy.

Shoulder to shoulder: with united effort.

Straight from the shoulder: a strong blow or strong criticism of someone.

To cold-shoulder someone: to ignore someone deliberately; treat coldly.

To have a chip on one's shoulder: to go around with a sense of grievance.

To have an old head on young shoulders: a young person who is wise beyond his age.

To have broad shoulders: to be strong; to be able to bear responsibility.

To put one's shoulder to the wheel: to make a great effort to do something.

To rub shoulders with: to mix with people.

To shoulder (a burden or the blame): to carry.

Skin

Skin-deep: (of beauty, emotion, wound), no deeper than the skin, not lasting, on the surface.

A skinflint: a mean, miserly person.

A skinhead: a member of a group of young people who have closely-cut hair, strange clothes and are often violent.

To be skin and bone: very thin.

To be thick-skinned: not to care what others say about one, insensitive.

To be thin-skinned: to be too sensitive to what others say.

To escape by the skin of one's teeth: to have a narrow escape.

To get under one's skin: to annoy intensely; to hold one's interest very much.

To jump out of one's skin: to be startled, frightened suddenly.

To keep one's eyes skinned: to be watchful.
To save one's skin: to avoid or escape from danger.
To skin: for a wound to be covered with new skin; to remove skin from something.

Skull

Thick-skulled: dull, stupid person.
To get something into one's skull: to understand and remember it.

Stomach

To have a strong stomach: ability not to feel nausea; can eat anything.
To have butterflies in the stomach: to have strange feelings in the stomach due to nervousness.
To stomach something: accept (usually in negative form). 'He cannot stomach her ways; cannot bear them.
To turn one's stomach: cause someone to be disgusted.

Teeth (see Tooth)

Throat

Cut-throat competition: fierce, intense struggle in business.
Throaty: guttural, spoken in the throat.
To cut one another's throats: to act in a way that harms both people.
To cut one's own throat: to act in a way that harms oneself; to kill oneself.
To have a frog in one's throat: hoarseness or loss of voice.
To have a lump in one's throat: to feel choked with emotion so that one can hardly speak.
To have a throat: to have a sore throat.
To have words stick in one's throat: to be too embarrassed by something to be able to speak of it.
To jump down someone's throat: to speak angrily to someone.
To thrust something down someone's throat: to try to make someone accept one's own beliefs, views, etc.

Thumb

A thumb-nail sketch: a short description.
Thumbs up!: mark of victory, satisfaction.
To be under someone's thumb: to be dominated by someone.
To thumb a lift: to sign with the thumb to ask a motorist for a free lift.
To twiddle one's thumbs: to have to sit still and do nothing.

Toe(s)

From top to toe: from head to foot, completely.
To be on one's toes: to be ready for action, alert.
To step/tread on someone's toes: to annoy someone unwittingly (often by doing what they want to do).
To tiptoe: to walk on the tips of one's toes.
To toe the line: to obey the rules, of a party, society, etc.
To turn up one's toes: to die.

Tongue

A slip of the tongue: a mistake made when speaking.
Tongue: language (e.g.) one's mother tongue: one's native language.
To be tongue-tied: to be too shy, too nervous to speak.
To have a dangerous tongue: to speak maliciously.
To have a long tongue: to be talkative.
To have a ready tongue: to speak easily, fluently.
To have something on the tip of one's tongue: to be about to say something and then forget it.
To hold one's tongue: to be silent.
To lose one's tongue: to be too shy to speak.
To put out one's tongue: grimace to mark displeasure; for doctor's inspection.
To speak with one's tongue in one's cheek: to say something which is not true in order to joke with someone.
To wag one's tongue to talk indiscreetly, to gossip.

Tooth, Teeth

In the teeth of evidence, opposition, wind, etc.: against it.

Teething troubles: difficulties in the first stages of something.

To be armed to the teeth: to be fully armed with many weapons.

To be fed up to the back teeth with something: to be bored by, tired of.

To be long in the tooth: to be old.

To cast something in someone's teeth: to blame him for it.

To cut a tooth: a new tooth begins to show above the gum (of babies and children).

To cut one's eye-teeth: to gain worldly wisdom, maturity.

To cut one's wisdom teeth: (as to cut one's eye-teeth).

To escape by the skin of one's teeth: to have a narrow escape.

To fight tooth and nail: to fight with all one's strength.

To get one's teeth into something: to make an enthusiastic start on a job, etc.

To have a sweet tooth: to enjoy eating sweet things.

To set one's teeth on edge: to cause an unpleasant feeling in the teeth; to cause disgust.

To show one's teeth: to become aggressive.

To take the bit between one's teeth: to reject the advice and control of others.

11 Language of dentistry

This chapter deals with the language used by patients when speaking about their teeth and the instructions the dentist gives. It is divided into five sections: (1) useful questions to patients; (2) colloquial language used by patients; (3) instructions to patients and explanations of procedures; (4) terms used in dentistry; (5) descriptive language.

USEFUL QUESTIONS TO PATIENTS

How long have you had the pain?
How long does the pain last?
Is it worse at night or in the day?
Does it disturb your sleep?
Where do you feel the pain most?
Have you pain in the temple or the ear?
Do you feel the pain when you touch your tooth with your tongue?
Do you get pain with cold or hot liquids?
Is the pain more severe when I press here or here?
Do your gums bleed when you brush your teeth?
Have you a feeling of weight in your tooth?
Have you ever had rheumatic fever, kidney disease, chest or lung diseases?
Have you any allergies — particularly penicillin allergy?
Have you been in hospital for anything?
Are you attending your doctor at present?
Are you taking any medicine?
Do you bleed a lot after extraction?

COLLOQUIAL LANGUAGE USED BY PATIENTS

The colloquial expression is shown in italics.
Decay: caries.
Gumboil: inflammation near decayed tooth; abscess.
Lower jaw: mandible.
Matter: pus.
Mattering: purulent.
Milk teeth: temporary teeth of children.
Pus from teeth sockets: pyorrhoea.
Proud flesh: excessive granulation tissue.
Redness: inflammation.
Roof of mouth: palate.
Upper jaw: maxilla.
Wisdom teeth: last molar teeth on each side of the jaw.

To cut one's teeth: expression used of babies' teeth.
To teeth: expression used of babies cutting their teeth.
To pull out a tooth: to extract, remove.
To stop a tooth: to fill a tooth.
My tooth is shaking: loose tooth (expression used by West Indian patients).
My gums are scratching: gums are sore (expression used by West Indian patients).

INSTRUCTIONS TO PATIENTS AND EXPLANATIONS OF PROCEDURES

Lean back.
Open your mouth wide.
Spit out.
Rinse your mouth well.
Please don't swallow.
Please keep still for a moment.
Unclench your teeth.
Clench your teeth.
Take out your plate/dentures.
Please don't close your mouth.

Your tooth is decayed. It must come out/be extracted.
This won't hurt you.
This may feel a little unpleasant.
This tooth is decayed. It needs filling.
This tooth will have to have a temporary/permanent filling.
Your teeth are crowded. I'll have to . . .
An abscess has formed. I'll have to open it up.
I'm going to remove the tartar from your teeth now.
I'm going to scrape your teeth and then polish them.
You must use a mouthwash every hour.
Take care not to touch the wound.
Do not rinse out your mouth for the rest of today.
I want you to paint the gums with . . .
Your gums are in poor condition. I want you to massage them and use dental floss or sticks.
Please don't have any solid food for a few days.
You must come every six months for a check-up and removal of tartar.

Language needed for anaesthesia

Local anaesthesia

Generally called: needle in the gum
                   prick in the gum.
You'll just feel a little prick in the gum.

General anaesthesia

Generally called: gas (inhalation anaesthesia)
                   prick in the arm (intravenous anaesthesia).
Sometimes referred to as 'go-to-sleep anaesthesia.'

Questions to patients

When did you last eat or drink?
Have you anyone with you?
Are you driving a car?

TERMS USED IN DENTISTRY

To apply a clamp.
To arrest bleeding.
To brush teeth.
To cap a tooth.
To cauterise.
To drill.
To extract a tooth (pull out, remove).
To file.
To fill.
To kill a nerve.
To plug a tooth.
To polish.
To put a gag in the mouth.
To remove the saliva by an ejector.
To rinse the cavity.
To scale.
To scrape.

An impacted tooth.
An unerupted tooth.
Premature teeth.
Retarded teeth.

Dentures

Dentures/artificial teeth/they're not my own teeth.
To take an impression.
To take the bite.
To grind off the artificial tooth until there is a perfect fit.
You must have a full set/top/bottom set.

DESCRIPTIVE LANGUAGE

Gums: anaemic, blackish, bleeding, buffy, dry, flabby, flaccid, hard,
  hot, inflamed, lacerated, livid, painful, pallid, ragged, raw,

reddened, rough, slack, smooth, soft, sore, spongy, swollen, tender, thickened, tight, turgid, ulcerous.

Teeth: crowded, decayed, defective, discoloured, elongated, eroded, irregularly placed, loosened, painful, sound.

Pain: see pages 179–180 for adjectives to describe pain.

12 Language of drug addiction

DRUG ADDICTION

Over the past few years, drug addiction has increased alarmingly, especially among the young. They are sometimes homeless and often buy drugs illegally. These young addicts have their own sub-culture and language, some of which has become widely used such as 'junkie', 'pusher' and 'hassle.' There are, however, local and regional words and phrases which may not be understood in different parts of the country. In the following glossary, these abbreviations are used: n, noun and v, verb.

Opioids: H, Horse, Junks, Shit, Skag, Smack, Stuff (Heroin), Morf (Morphine), Phy, Phy pills, Amps, Linctus (all Methadone), Dike (Diconal), Palf (Palfium), DFs (DF 118), Peth (Pethidine), Fortral (Fortral).

Stimulants: Nikki, Nose, Nose candy, Speed (amphetamine, methylamphetamine, methedrine), Dex, Dexies (Dexedrine), Sulph (Amphetamine Sulphate), Pep Pills (stimulants), Prellies (Preludin), Blues, Bluies (blue amphetamine pills), C, Charlie, Coke, Crack, Snow (Cocaine), Meth (Methedrine, etc.), uppers (stimulants), Rit (Ritalin, methentermine).

Other sedatives: Barbs (barbiturates), Tuies (Tuinal), Nembies (Nembutal), Seckies (Seconal), Amytal (Amytal), Mogies (Mogadon), Libs, Green and Blacks (Librium), Ciba's (Doriden), Knockout drops, Mickey Finn (Chloral Hydrate), Ludes (Quaaludes, methaqualone), Mandies (Mandrax), Downers,

Sleepers (depressants), Hem, Heminev (Heminevrin), Red Chicken (Heroin on a barbiturate base), Vals (Valium).

Psychedelics: Acid, a tab of acid (LSD), Dots (microdots, LSD), Ecstasy, Ginseng (a mild Chinese psychedelic, not controlled), Lucey, Mushrooms (Psilocybin), Peace pills, STP (serenity, tranquillity, peace).

Cannabis/Marijuana: Hash, Lebanese gold, Acapulco gold (high quality cannabis), Sausage, THC, Resin (cannabis), Brick (kilo of compressed marijuana), Dope, Mary Jane, Pot, Weed, Tea, Grass (all marijuana), Ganga (West Indian hashish), Joint, Smoke, Blo, (cannabis cigarettes), Roach (the end part of a joint containing the cardboard support), Mellow (dried banana skins for smoking). Seeds, pearly gates (morning glory seeds).

Marijuana cigarette: African woodbine, Drag, Joint, Joystick, Reefer, Roach — end of cigarette, Sausage (Musicians), Smoke, Spliff, Stick. Blast party: group of marijuana smokers smoking together. Blast a stick: smoke a marijuana cigarette. Blow a stick: as above. Block: black market term for ounce of hashish (resin). Burn (n): a solitary minor smoking of marijuana. Deal: small amount of cannabis. Manicure: clean and prepare marijuana for rolling into cigarettes. Pot-head: marijuana user. Rolling-up: making a marijuana cigarette. Skins: papers to roll joints and make reefers or joints with. Smoke (v): to smoke marijuana cigarette. Stoned: marijuana effect. Teahead: user of marijuana. Turn on (v): to smoke a marijuana cigarette. Weed Heads: marijuana users. Wrap up: brown paper packet containing cannabis.

DRUG TAKERS: THEIR EQUIPMENT, HABITS, ETC.

Amp: ampoule, a container of dangerous drugs.

Arrow: injection equipment.

Bad hit: an undesirable effect after taking drug.

Barbed up: intoxication with barbiturates.

Binge, going on a: to go on an intensive period of drug taking.

Brew up: prepare an injection

Burn (v): to take someone else's narcotic and not return it, to smoke (mainly marijuana).

Cap: capsule of narcotics.

Carry (n): a load of drugs.

Chasing the dragon: (a form of free-basing) heating heroin on tinfoil and inhaling fumes.

Clean: recovered from drug dependence.

Connection: dealer in narcotics.

Crank up: to inject a narcotic.

Cut: adulterate narcotics.

Dealer: person from whom drugs are obtained.

Dirty fix: unhygienic injection.

Doctor Scrip: a doctor who easily prescribes drugs.

Doobs: pills.

Dope: any narcotics.

Drop (v): to swallow a pill.

Drug free: recovered from drug dependence.

Fix (n): an injection.

Fix (v): to inject a drug.

Flushing: drawing blood back into syringe and injecting back into vein.

Free-basing: method of purifying street drugs (e.g. chasing the dragon, smoking crack).

Gear: addict's drug.

Glue-sniffing: practice of inhaling vapour from glue and other volatile substances such as butane gas, petrol, etc.

Guide: someone familiar with drugs and relatively sober while others try it for the first time.

Habit: addiction to drugs with physical dependence; dosage commonly taken.

Hard stuff: cocaine and opiates.

Hippy: drug user, especially psychedelic.

Hit: experience.

Hooked: addicted to drugs.

Hustling: buying drugs.

Jack up: take an injection of a narcotic.

John: lavatory, place for injecting.

Junkie: heroin taker.

Load (n): stock of illegal drugs.

Loaded: full of drugs.

M.: morphine.

Main-lining: injecting intravenously.

Middle man: dealer in narcotics.

Mumbling: conning or tricking the doctor.

Needle: addict's syringe, etc.

Okay scene: enjoyable drug party.

On look out: searching for drugs.

Pill head: person on pills, usually amphetamine type.

Pop: inject.

Popping: subcutaneous injection of a drug.

Pusher: person who sells drugs illegally and tries to induce people to start taking them.

Quill: folded matchbox cover for sniffing narcotics through the nose.

Registered: obtain regular prescription for drugs.

Rip off (v): to smoke.

Rumble: police in the neighbourhood; a search for drugs.

Runner: drug supplier.

Scene: place where people meet to take drugs, group of users of drugs, particular group of people.

Score (v): to obtain drugs.

Scrip, Script: a prescription for drugs.

Set of works: addict's syringe, etc.

Shoot up: take an injection.

Shooting gallery: place where addicts meet to shoot up.

Shot: an injection.

Sink (v): to swallow a pill.

Skin-popping: subcutaneous or intramuscular injection.

Sniff (v), Snort (v): to sniff narcotics through nose, usually heroin or cocaine.

Spike: hypodermic needle.

Stash: hiding place for narcotics.

Stuff: any narcotics.

Supplier: drug source.

Suss out: police search for drugs.

Tabs: tablet form of drugs, usually LSD.

Tie up: tourniquet used to prepare vein for injection.

Tools: addict's apparatus.
Turn on (v): to give a non-addict his first shot.
Turned on: under the influence of drugs.
User: taker of drugs, mainly narcotic.
Works: addict's apparatus.

LANGUAGE USED TO EXPRESS EFFECTS OF DRUG TAKING

Bang, Buzz, Flash, Rush: sensation experienced after injecting a narcotic intravenously.
Be heavy, serious (v): to be heavily addicted.
Blocked: being under the influence of a drug (particularly drinamyl).
Blow your mind (v): to enter into a frenzied state of mind.
Brought down (v): to be elated and then suddenly unexpectedly depressed.
Bummer: unpleasant experience, especially with LSD.
Come down (v): to lose drug-induced exhilaration as it wears off.
Crash: sleep, pass out from drugs.
Experience: LSD or mescaline experience.
Flake out (v): to lose consciousness.
Flash: effect of cocaine; to lesser extent of methedrine.
Freak out: psychedelic happening.
High: feeling good; state of euphoria after taking drugs.
Horrors: acute unpleasant drug effects: (i) cocaine or amphetamine psychosis; (ii) acute withdrawal.
Nod (to nod, on the nod): drowsy state following injection of narcotics.
Psychedelic experience: effect of LSD or other hallucinogen.
Raver: person under influence of excessive amount of amphetamine.
Red eye: refers to conjunctival infection. May occur after use of marijuana.
Spaced out: out of touch with reality.
Taste (a taste of): taking a small amount of a drug and having little reaction.
Track marks: signs of injection in veins.
Trip: effect of LSD or other hallucinogen.

LANGUAGE OF WITHDRAWAL

Cleaned out, Dried out: drug free, to have taken a 'cure'.
Cold turkey: Abrupt withdrawal of narcotics. Derived from appearance of skin — usually called 'goose flesh'.
Detox: give up drugs.
Drying out: slow withdrawal from narcotics.
Hung up: unable to get drugs, depressed, let down, disappointed.
Kicking the habit: stopping drugs.
Munchies: to eat excessively when being withdrawn from narcotics.
Sick: narcotic drug withdrawal symptoms.
Strung out: feeling ill from lack of narcotics or other hard drugs.

GENERAL SLANG USED BY ADDICTS

(Slang word in bold type)

Bad scene: unpleasant surroundings, bad situation, bad vibrations.
Big house, in the: in prison.
Bird, 'to do bird': to serve a prison sentence.
Bread: money.
Bull: detective.
Bum: tramp.
Bust (v) (busted): to arrest (to be arrested).
CID: detective.
Clean: off narcotics, not carrying drugs at that time.
Cop out: confess.
Derry: derelict house.
Freak: a long-haired drug user.
Fuzz: police.
Gas: terrific, marvellous.
Grass: informer.
Groovy: up-to-date, beautiful, good.
Hang up: personal problem.
Hassle: inconvenience, nuisance.
Heavy: important, serious.
Heeled: possessing drugs.
Hot: wanted by police.

Kip (v) (**to have a kip**): sleep (not always rough).

Law: policeman.

Man: police authority.

Meths: methylated spirits.

Nicked: arrested.

Old Bill: policeman.

Pad: room, or apartment.

Pig: policeman.

Plain clothes: detective.

Porridge: prison term.

Rat: to go back on a bargain or inform on someone.

Red Biddy: methylated or surgical spirits in wine (N. Ireland).

Rip off: sell weak or non-narcotic substances as hard drugs.

Road: on the road, vagabond life.

Rumble: police nearby.

Shrink: psychiatrist (head shrinker).

Skippering: travelling about with one's belongings, bedding down with others.

Sleep rough: sleep anywhere.

Square: conventional, old-fashioned, not 'with-it'.

Squat: illegal occupation of premises.

Stash: hide drugs.

Stool: informer.

Straight: ordinary tobacco cigarettes; a non-drug user.

Time (**doing time**): to serve a prison sentence.

turn over (v): to rob.

Uptight: angry, tense, worried.

i 1333 8377